SMELLING THE ROSES
Memoir Of An Irish Philosopher

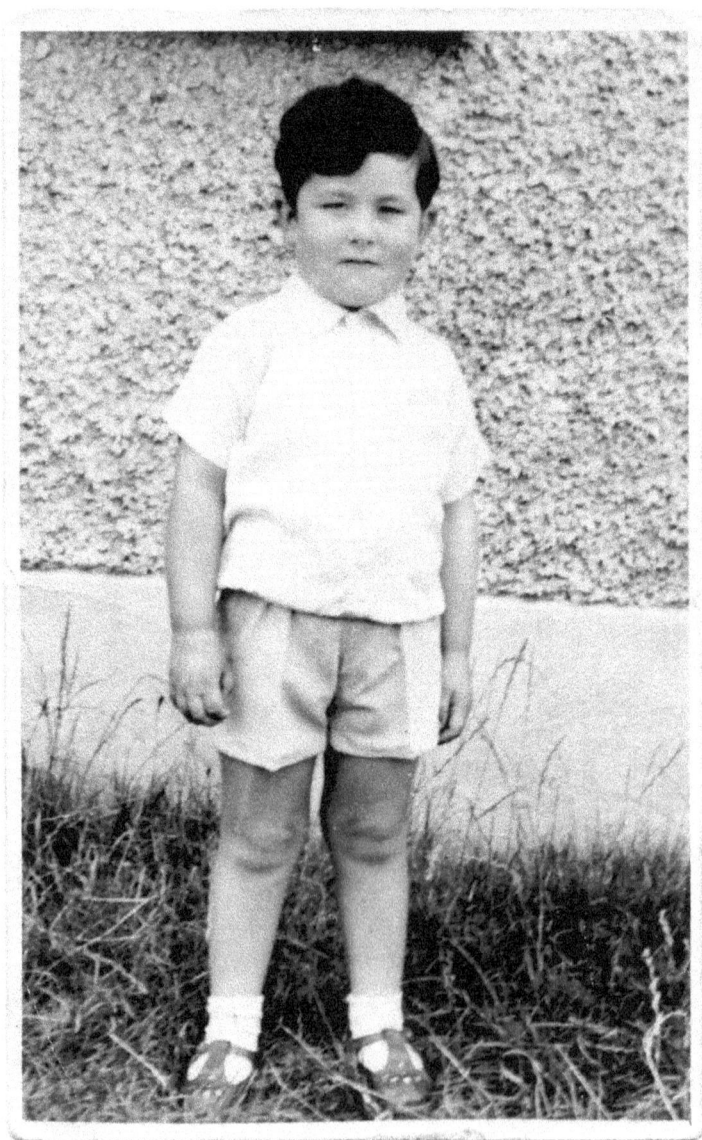

Mervyn, age 6, in his Sunday best.

SMELLING THE ROSES
Memoir Of An Irish Philosopher

Mervyn J. Brady

SMELLING THE ROSES
Memoir Of An Irish Philosopher

Inquiries should be addressed to:

Academy of European Arts and Culture
7513 New Salem Street
San Diego, CA 92126-2009

information@academyofeuropeanarts.com

The Academy of European Arts and Culture
First Printing 2013

ISBN-13: 978-0615737737
ISBN-10: 0615737730

Cover Design by Ollie Weait
Layout & Compilation by Jenny Holloway
Editing by Lisa Cahn

Printed in the United States of America

The Academy of European Arts and Culture
is a 501(c)(3) non-profit organization.

To Mervyn's Children -

Thank you for sharing your father with so many.
We dedicate this book to you.

*"Writing this book has given me such joy as I continually verify
that almost my entire childhood was magic and beautiful."*

*"I vowed to guard my children's childhood for them
and not to speed them into the world of adults and the body.
I promised myself that I would talk to them about fairies, angels
and leprechauns, and all the strange and wonderful creatures who
share this splendid world in another place, very close to us.
Within the openhearted wonder of a child
lies the key to heaven."*

M.B.

CONTENTS

FOREWARD

This book is a collection of Mervyn's childhood stories that he wrote between 1998 and 1999. A few other writings, from his vast body of work, have also been selected to give you a glimpse of his adult life and teachings. Most of what follows is in Mervyn's own words. Sprinkled throughout, however, are the words and stories of some of his students about their interactions with him.

All great love must be shared. We want to share with you our love for our teacher and great friend, Mervyn Brady. He was an extraordinary man who had the steadfast courage and great desire to live for his Soul.

INTRODUCTION TO MERVYN
BY HOLLY

Mervyn Brady was our spiritual teacher and guide, friend and confidant. An enlightened person is patient, powerful and wise. He was all that, but the most beautiful thing about Mervyn was that he was imperfect. So perfectly imperfect. Human. He was not a sheltered saint. He was real. His wisdom and his understanding came from a big Soul that lived a very big life.

To some, he seemed an unlikely candidate for spiritual awakening, but if you shared a moment with him, you experienced his extraordinary being. Mervyn's presence radiated warmth that stilled the incessant thoughts in your head, and then, a quiet light found a way into your heart. Afterward, it wasn't unusual to wonder what had happened. But something in you had been deeply, undeniably transformed.

Later in his life, he suffered a hip injury that made walking difficult for him, but he never stopped traveling across three continents to be with his students. He would tell us, "You're the luckiest bastards – to have the teacher travel to you." And it's true. We were the luckiest bastards in the world.

Once, I heard him muse, "Why would God awaken me, an overweight, unhealthy man who walks in pain?"

In Mervyn, God found a Soul with the enormous desire and courage to love and to live this life. Most people cower in the face of love, and, afraid of their vulnerabilities, they doom themselves to little lives. In Mervyn, God found a worthy vessel to experience his creation.

Mervyn was full of contradictions, but his big Soul and big heart were able to hold all of them. He devoted himself entirely to the Highest, but he was also irreverent and wickedly funny. He had a wonderful sense of humor that lightened serious discussions so that his message could reach the heart. He knew how to silently navigate around our vulnerabilities, often mercifully ignoring our falseness and bravado. Then a certain glance would tell you that he knew and loved you all the same. He was kind and gracious, but he could be fierce and uncompromising, especially in protection of his inner world and his school. This powerful combination of commanding presence and magnetic warmth made him a gifted speaker. He could hold a lecture for an audience of fifty with the ease and intimacy of a private conversation. But most remarkable was his ability to create a special bond with everyone in his life. He gave a unique part of himself to each of us.

Mervyn passed away in April 2006. Our enormous sorrow over his passing and our love for Mervyn has drawn us closer to each other. With our memories of Mervyn deep in our hearts, we celebrate his Soul and honor his life by carrying forward the Great Work that he began.

HIS TEACHINGS

Mervyn taught the Fourth Way system (practical and sacred knowledge from different esoteric teachings, compiled and integrated by G.I. Gurdjieff), to lay the foundation for inner work and provide us with tools to understand the machine*, the physical body with its emotions and intellect. The need to communicate the sensitive experiences of the inner world means that a common language is necessary. But when Mervyn awoke, he spoke the words of the Christian mystics: St. John of the Cross, St. Theresa of Avila, Meister Eckhart. In their words he found the language of the Soul, of Divine Love.

Mervyn recognized that the processes of awakening and love are the same. He devoted his later years to teaching

---

* The machine is the physical body, the emotional body and the intellectual body. The inner, non-physical self is the Soul. There is a higher emotional and intellectual body that experiences the Soul, but most of the time we are not in touch with this.

about love. He saw that it is in those rare moments of real love that our Souls emerge; and in that moment we know with absolute certainty that we are much greater than we know. And like an addiction, entire lives are spent trying to reach those moments of love again. Love is a difficult subject because it quickly becomes a cliche with all the sentimentality and loaded agendas mixed up with the undeniable truth. But it is in light of Divine Love that we find our path back to home: the path that we lost in the flash and confusion of our lives. Inside us, in that most quiet place, lies the path to love and awakening. It's the most difficult journey of all because it's an invisible journey within, in which we are asked to become what we already are.

* * *

1

INTRODUCTION TO MY LIFE

Dear All,

These extracts are true.

I share them with you because when I awoke it was not strange to me. I knew I had been awake before. To my astonishment I saw that I was awake as a child and it was a wonderful experience to revisit my life. These observations are real and I have tried to speak in the language of the child at various ages.

Love,
Mervyn 1999

INTRODUCTION TO MY LIFE

"If I tried to express what my Soul thought,
Willy nilly,
Even should I have twenty tongues?
I would sound dumb and silly."
--Author unknown

I was born in Dublin, Ireland, in the sitting room of my parents' house. The year was 1948 and my weight was twelve pounds. My mother had been told to expect twins and was greatly relieved when just one great big lump of a kid was born.

"Jesus Christ, look at the size of him!" were the words that greeted me as I came into this world and which would plague me for the rest of my life.

Apparently, for the first year all I did was sleep and guzzle milk from my mother. She said she loved me so much that she used to nudge me awake just so I would smile at her. It was a love relationship that would last the next forty-eight years.

After six months, she supplemented my diet with bottles of Cow and Gate baby formula, occasionally mixed with Guinness, which she insisted would build me up. It was quite common in those days in Ireland for a mother to mix Guinness with milk. In fact, I think pregnant mothers were officially encouraged to drink a couple of bottles of the stuff every day.

I had an older sister, Madeleine, and for the first four years of my life we lived in Farney Park, which was in a lovely part of Dublin called Sandymount. My first real memory of this life gave me such a shock that I still remember it today. Apparently, I was crawling around the floor and stuck my finger in an electric socket. There was a big bang. Then my mother and father came running into the room.

"Jesus, Mary and Joseph! Where's the child gone?"

I had been shot under the bed by the sheer force of whatever happened. To this day, I can still see my parents' feet running around the bedroom like headless chickens looking for me.

"Look under the fucken' bed, why don't ya?"

I remember thinking that I knew they would eventually find me, so there was no need to panic. I can still see my mother's head appearing under the bed and hearing the relief in her voice.

"Jesus! He's under the bed, the little brat!"

Isn't it strange that doctors say our brains don't develop the ability to speak until after the age of two, yet when we remember our earliest thoughts, they're not in jibberish like "babagoogoogoo"? My infant self was thinking in words.

Maybe our Souls can speak and it just takes time for our mouths to learn to talk. After all, I had already been in my mother for nine months, and my Soul must have picked up the lingo while it was hanging around waiting to be born. That's where it probably learned to swear like an Irishwoman and say things like, "look under the fucken' bed!"

I didn't think in baby talk. I knew things, but I just didn't know how to say them. Or maybe I had no reason to say them because nobody asked me. I was just fine guzzling my milk and Guinness, like a little cherub, perfectly happy in my own paradise.

Then something went seriously wrong. People and kids started talking to me, telling me all sorts of things. And, worse, I started to listen. The resulting confusion is what this book is all about. And if I was confused, you probably were too. In the words of Harry, my first great sage and mentor, "the electricity probably damaged your fucken' brain."

* * *

2

LEARNING THE RULES OF THE GAME

When a human is born, there is a body and a Soul. Until the age of three, the body and Soul exist side-by-side. After age three, we start saying "I." We learn to become a child. If you have memories before the age of three, you'll realize that those thoughts are profoundly vivid, the perceptions of a fully developed mind, not those of a very young child. But then the notion of "I" begins. My name is Mervyn, I am Irish, that's my father, that's my brother, that's my house. The body starts to grow; it goes to school and becomes educated, receiving more information about who it is supposed to be – Jewish or Christian or Japanese. And that's where our sense of I, our identity, our personality, comes from.

Soon we forget about the Soul that is inside us. The body starts to eclipse the Soul the way the little moon eclipses the entire sun. The body blocks the Soul. And because the Soul is no longer recognized, it slowly goes into hibernation, just as the body will shut down if it is no longer fed. By the tender age of seven, the Soul is already asleep.

Throughout history, many schools of philosophy knew this. Most fairytales were created to remind children of their Souls. Monasteries took in children before they were seven years old so they could catch these Souls before they went to sleep.

It's not easy being in a body. Once we were free, boundless. Now we must learn how to use these bodies to navigate through the world. It's a weird and crazy place; no wonder the Soul wants to retreat back into the warm confines of the body.

-- Excerpt from "The Divine Art of Self-remembering," Lecture in New York City, 2005.

THE BRADY MONASTERY

At about the age of five, I was fated to meet Harry Kennedy on our street. One of the great things about the Irish is that they sure can talk. Sure, there's nothing much else to do but talk, sharing half-formed ideas with each other; but Harry was something special. He had wisdom and knowledge like no one else, and all the kids on our road quickly became a readymade bunch of disciples.

Until I met Harry, I had put in five years of hard time at the "Brady Monastery," learning all about my body functions and how to control them. Like most of us, I don't have much memory of this time. Maybe it's because nothing very interesting happened. After all, how exciting can eating and expelling at an ever-increasing rate really be?

The process from crawling to walking took longer than average for me; I would rather guzzle milk than squirm my way, for no apparent reason, to the other side of the room. Have you noticed that some babies are born with the desire to crawl everywhere and end up hurting themselves by trying to walk before their time? Well, that wasn't the case with me. Many years later my mother told me that she loved my fat little legs and would feed me a bit extra so I wouldn't get scrawny like the kid next door.

Up until the age of five or so, apart from thinking with a Dublin accent, my environment didn't have a big impact on me. I suppose childhood is the same everywhere - learning the basics like toilet training, playing nice with my sisters and not throwing food. It's funny that at this stage we learn all the things that make us good boys and girls.

Then one day I heard the word "school" and was told that I was going to spend a long, long time in one. As it does for many of us, this one word forever changed my whole lovely existence of guzzling and motherly love. Born into a world of endless love and affection, I would now be "born again" into the crazy world of my Dublin childhood.

WALKING TO SCHOOL IN THE WINTER

Nothing creates the feeling of solitude as much as walking alone in the rain, hearing it beat down on your oilskin hat. These were always great moments for reflection. I used to walk past an old graveyard on the way home and think of death. The smell of the wet grass filling the air often made me think of the people below, cozy in their graves. I couldn't come to terms with the fact that when you die, you no longer exist. Somehow I sensed they were all still there in the graveyard, maybe envious of me in my healthy body strolling about.

On days when it was very cold, me ma prepared hard-boiled eggs for my sisters and me, one in each pocket, to keep us warm. Sometimes, when I couldn't find my gloves, I would use an odd pair of socks on my hands for the two-mile walk to school. As I got colder, I took the gloves off so the eggs could warm my hands better. Then at lunchtime, I would eat them. Sometimes it got so cold that when you got a bottle of milk in the playground at lunchtime, you had to stick your finger through the cream on the top because it would freeze. Then you had to hold the bloody frozen bottle in your hand and drink it. If we got a long spell of cold weather, we'd get fed up eating eggs and throw them out behind the school. We were always getting told off for this because one of the Brothers would have to go out with a big broom and sweep them up.

Big trays of sandwiches would be left out, and you had to queue up for one. On Monday it was cheese, Tuesday, corned beef, Wednesday, jam, Thursday, corned beef again. And on Friday, jam again. We used to wonder why they didn't give us fish on Fridays, but Harry explained that you can't get a fish into a sandwich.

Harry could answer any question I ever had. He knew so much and even when he was dead wrong he would start to shout really loud, arguing his point so fiercely, that despite any doubts I might have had, I believed him. Of course later, when I got a bit wiser, I realized there were thousands of Harrys out there, just waiting to show me the way. But right now, this Harry had all the answers.

One day he fascinated us with his knowledge of science. Derek Shannon said he had a headache, and Harry explained that was because he was holding back his farts.

"When you do that, gas goes up into your head – gas rises, right? – and gives you a headache."

We'd all watch Derek try really hard to fart so he could get rid of his headache, all the while Harry egging him on.

Everything Harry said always made so much sense. His air of confidence made him sound right even when he was completely wrong. He told me I was fat because I was full of water and didn't piss enough. So I stopped drinking for a long time to get my backlog of piss out. When I pointed out that not drinking water didn't make me any less fat, he explained

I had an internal blockage. Jesus, there wasn't anything he didn't know. I faithfully referred to my "blockage" for years, and to this day, I wonder if Harry wasn't right.

Harry was the first and last authority on all our questions. He even knew about questions we asked someone else; he would explain how the other fella was wrong, even before he knew what the other fella meant. Harry was something else. He was the tallest of all the lads. He had a big skull, long hands and feet. I used to secretly call him "the Bone Man," but I never dared to tell anyone. He spoke really slowly, like John Wayne. And he enunciated everything. He didn't just speak; he enunciated. When he looked at you, you felt guilty even if you hadn't done anything wrong.

Somehow he represented all the rules. He always knew what was right and wrong, and everybody sided with him even when they knew, deep down, that they were right. He took everything he said very seriously. When you asked him a question he would frown and think real hard. Sometimes I would get pissed off waiting, while he worked out the answer.

THE PLAYGROUND

On the playground, I encountered a whole new world. I entered the playground innocent and full of trust, believing that everything I was told was for my own good. Until then, me ma had been my only authority figure; she told me everything I needed to know and answered all my questions. But even at that young age, on the playground, there were those who felt they knew everything; and I admired and revered anyone who knew more than I.

There, I discovered all different species of humans. There were those skinny, gangly ones who spent the whole lunch hour bouncing and running around, like demented springs. At times they'd come to a screeching stop in front of me and say in amazement, "You're a fucken' fat bastard, aren't ya." That would confuse me because I had been standing there, in full sight, for a long time. Then one would check with each other and say, "He is, isn't he? A big, fat bastard." The scrawnier one would agree, and they'd stare at me for a few more seconds. Then, as if by some invisible signal, they'd run off.

I loved several of the older girls on the playground and wanted to marry them, if I could only figure out how to get one. There was one girl who kept shoving and pushing me; I knew she liked me. She'd smile at me, and when I'd smile back at her, she'd whack me on the shoulder really hard. I didn't understand what was happening, but I knew that one day I would kiss her. And I did.

And there were the real bastards, sent from hell, who'd pick on everyone. There was always someone else, thank God, who cried from their abuse. Somehow that appeased those bastards.

THE SCHOOL BAND

Our school band consisted of over forty accordion players and two drummers, and I was one of the drummers. Brother Cypriot would point out notes on the board with his cane. If he heard one wrong note from one of those forty accordions, he'd yell "Stop!" hold his head in pain, and scream horrible things at us. Forty boys with accordions, instruments larger than some of us, would tremble in case they were the tone deaf culprit. Brother Cypriot would leap over the seats and scream at the victim so hard his face would turn red, and then he would make the poor boy play it again. Sure enough, when the terrified boy repeated the same mistake, he'd get a smack on the ear or a whack on the fingers with the cane.

I knew I was protected by a guardian angel, whom I very often thanked for guiding me to the drums, because Brother Cypriot couldn't play the drums and therefore wasn't as sensitive to my mistakes. I couldn't really play the drums, but somehow he never realized it.

I learned quickly how each boy would take the insults and whacks and forget it, however unreasonable and cruel the unbridled bullying and punishments were. But again my guardian angel was looking out for me because in all the years we spent together, Brother Cypriot never once raised his voice to me.

He was an outrageous flirt with women, and one day I caught him with the nun in the bandwagon. This time he was the one who looked worried. He must have been relieved when I quietly closed the door, pretending not to see him. From that day on, we had an unspoken understanding. Perhaps we somehow acknowledged each other's humanity.

THE BENT FENCE

Each day after school, over one thousand children poured out of the school's main gate, scattering like cockroaches in every direction. I made my way home with the kids from my street, and braced myself for my daily humiliation. The kids took a shortcut through the park. Surrounding the park was a big iron fence, but there was a place where two rails had been bent apart, and the kids would squeeze through it, one by one. Everyone, that is, except me. I was too fat.

Every now and then, some good-natured bastard would take it on himself to sort out my problem. It normally went like this:

"Okay, Fatser, put your left leg through first, now, your head. That's it." Then a guy who was already inside the rails would take my hand and start pulling, and, of course, I'd get stuck. "Wait a minute! He still has his fucken' schoolbag on."

This was encouraging to them because now they thought they'd finally discovered the great secret of getting me through the fence. So off came the schoolbag from my back, and the process was repeated. With renewed vigor, they'd try to shove and yank me through. But, once again, I'd get stuck. "Take your fucken' overcoat off!" Then it'd be my jacket. And I'd get stuck again. By this point they'd give up and I'd wiggle myself out and take the long walk around the park.

But one day after a particularly vigorous bout, the

bastards had me down to my vest, and when they got me halfway through, I was really stuck. I knew I was in trouble because I couldn't go forward or backward, so I began to curse like a trooper.

"I told you I didn't fit, ya stupid bastards!" I roared, as I squirmed like a pig. I was half naked and stuck. And the crowd started to get bigger as the kids poured out of the school.

"Hey look! There's a fat cunt stuck in the railings!"

I was dying of shame and boiling with rage at these bloody, no-good Samaritans. It was in this condition, while howling with indignation in my vest, when Harry and a kid named Damien came along. As usual, Harry immediately took charge and pushed all the kids back. Then he started to think. Praise God! I knew everything was going to be all right; Harry was thinking.

Everybody went quiet to let him think. After what seemed like ages, he spoke.

"Has anybody got any milk?"

"What the fuck do ya want milk for?' shouted a fella in the crowd.

"Sure, isn't he fat enough as he is?"

They all roared with laughter.

"For lubrication, ya eegit!" retorted Harry with a look of contempt.

What the fuck is lubrication? I asked myself silently as someone produced a bottle of milk from a schoolbag.

Then Harry poured the bloody freezing milk all over me. To this day, I'll never quite understand what happened, but I think the shock of the freezing milk must have temporarily shrunk me or something, because I shot out of the fence in one big jump.

I'll never forget the fellas' faces as they stared, dumbfounded, at Harry. Harry was incredible! How did he know it would work?

But I was drenched in milk, freezing, and trying to dry my hair with my jacket.

"What am I going to say to me ma when I arrive home drenched in milk?"

"Ah, tell her you were attacked by a mad cow!" shouted some smartass in the crowd.

More roars of laughter.

Humiliated, I set off alone down the road, while the others piled through the gap in the fence, laughing and jeering at me. I hated those bastards who tried to solve my "problem." Who says it was a problem, anyway? I had become accustomed to walking home on my own and actually looked forward to a bit of peace from the incessant chatter of fifty kids. It was during these times that I learned to appreciate solitude. Sometimes I thought God was unfair for not letting me through the gap, but it was a blessing in disguise; it created that distinct feeling of being different, close to something higher. I began to understand that when you're deeply hurt, something enters your blood and silently changes you.

On the walk home that day, a miracle of sorts happened. Suddenly, without any warning, I felt like I was floating. The hard concrete of the pavement seemed to transform into a huge feather cushion. The grass in the park was beautiful, and I could smell it. I was amazed that I was looking down at myself walking along. One part of me was watching in astonishment, while the other was in a kind of ecstasy. I could hear my body breathing, in and out, in and out, and I knew that my body was not the real me; somehow, I had arrived at a place I knew I should be. But when I turned the corner toward home, it brought me back into my body, and this beautiful state of being ended.

But the Mervyn who turned the corner that day was not the one who came out the other side. Even though I was back in my body, I knew from that moment on that I was different. The pain and humiliation from earlier in the day had transformed, and I was no longer sad and angry. It was actually kind of funny. Even the thought of going to school the next day didn't bother me.

When I got home, my mother asked me why my vest was covered in milk. I just smiled and told her how much I appreciated her. She was such a beautiful person. Often, she'd just hug me and tell me what a strange boy I was. She'd tell me that she had faith in God and that He knew what He was doing.

As fate would have it, the biggest milk company in

Dublin at the time was called "Merville Dairies," so by the next day in school I had a new name, "Merville Dairies." Fortunately, news about the incident centered on Harry's brilliance, rather than on the fat kid that got stuck in the fence.

Derek Shannon claimed that Harry didn't actually come up with that solution; Harry was just copying his da. Derek further explained that one day in his front garden he saw two dogs with their arses stuck together.

"What the fuck are you talking about, Shannon? How can two dogs' arses get stuck together?

"Yeah, they can," said Patsy Whealan.

Several of the fellas solemnly agreed. The rest of us were amazed.

"Anyway," continued Derek, "me da came out and threw a bucket of freezing water over them, and they became unstuck."

We were all puzzled by the unsticking powers of freezing liquids, when Harry entered the conversation.

"We know where you got the idea to free Merville Dairies from the railings," said Patsy knowingly. "It's what they do to unstick dogs' arses when they're stuck, right?"

Harry looked at Patsy as if he were a piece of a shite. "What, in Jesus' name are ya rattling on about?" Harry was almost shouting now. "I poured the milk over him because of the FAT. So it would lubricate him, you dope!"

We didn't say anything. When Harry left, I turned to

Patsy and asked him what "lubricate" meant.

"I don't know," answered Patsy, "but it has something to do with you being fat."

"Can people get their arses stuck?" I asked.

"Of course they can. Isn't that how babies are made?"

DE LA SALLE

"Do not ignore my eyes or hairy face
For in this skull a Soul has found its place."
-- Author unknown

One year it was decided that we would give a drill display. Almost one thousand boys, dressed in white trousers and white shirts, were forced to march in different formations. When we were in our final positions, we knelt and bent forward, our faces touching our knees – not an easy position for me. Then an airplane flew over the sports field and took an aerial photo of us. We spelled out the name of the order of Christian brothers who taught us: DE LA SALLE. I was on the tip of the D.

A few days later at school, a bunch of my friends were laughing and pointing at a huge photo of the arial shot.

"Jesus, Fatser! Come over here and have a look at yourself!"

I saw the school's name spelled out. And there I was on the top of the D. Twice the size of all the other white dots.

* * *

STUDENT STORY: ABIGAIL

I had just turned 32 when I met the school in August 2000, and I joined in October. A few weeks later, Mervyn arrived. We met at a coffee shop. I went to hug Mervyn; his face and smile reminded me of Santa Claus. I loved his name. I called him Merlin for several months and no one corrected me. I sat next to him, perhaps he motioned me to do so, and found my head on his chest, under his arm (a spot I visited many times over the next six years) and soon fell asleep while he led a group around us. The sleep was so peaceful, as if I was curled up under the most beautiful, familiar, ancient, wise, loving tree that would protect me for ever and ever... I was home.

I do not remember when I realized that Mervyn "saw" me. I knew it though. It was this that kept me in school. To be seen – to be truly seen – somehow validated my existence. Loaded with emotions and meaning, this was my wish all of my life. And here I had found it. The search was over.

This was the first time I called someone a teacher despite the fact that I had attended other spiritual groups. A teacher to me is someone who teaches by their action, someone who is real, someone who sees me and can contain all of me, who is bigger than I am, who can show me the real me. Someone who can see and experience so much more, so I have something to look forward to, to learn from. To be seen, and to be unconditionally loved once fully seen—that is love.

It is because of Mervyn that I started to appreciate my "stay" on earth, my bodily existence, and felt I had room on this earth, with another person, and even a group. Wonder why I love this man, this soul? He reflected love that I had only felt from those on the other side!

And now, you, dear soul travelers, you reflect and love this soul and body, as our teacher once did and still does from the other side. The healing in that reflection has saved me…I hear Amazing Grace in my head… I once was lost and now I am found. Thank you, dearest Mervyn, for making this journey enjoyable and for so much more… words are too restricting to describe my gratitude and love. You feel it.

Love You Across Forever,
Abigail

* * *

3
HIGHER STATES

Higher states, anything we wish to understand, can be understood or answered by "The Teachers" (the Gods). Anywhere one wishes to visit can be visited and anyone one wishes to meet can be found.

I had been a spectator of everything and nothing. The great Wise Silence had visited me again, and I knew I had been changed again. One is always different when one returns.

The Sun was completely gone now and everything had descended into the darkness of night, when all living things are refreshed.

For my Soul there was no end place.

Perhaps I will be the "Wise Silent" answer to your next perplexing question, or the cause of your smile.

One thing is sure, keep your eyes and ears peeled, I am out there in the Universe somewhere and You might be part of the next Adventure.

Email to Academy, June 2002

SMELLING THE ROSES

In the center of Dublin lies St. Stephen's Green. I loved catching a bus to O'Connell Street and walking up Grafton Street to the Green. This was a place where you could really see life, in particular the kind of people you'd never find where I lived. There were always gypsy women standing outside the gates with little sprigs of heather wrapped in silver paper. They wrapped big blankets around their bodies, and usually a snotty nosed kid peered out from somewhere inside the blanket. They instinctively knew who was a tourist, who was kind, generous or weak.

In spring, the gypsies sold "lucky heather" flowers. Speaking of luck, how lucky and happy the ducks were... rich Americans were lucky too. They only had to figure out what to spend money on next. I envied them. Sometimes they'd talk to me, and I wondered how to become one. My family was fine, but these people had seen and been to places that I only dreamed of. They gave me glimpses into a different world; my life was full of glimpses, but never a real good look.

There were all sorts of rules you had to obey in the park, or else one of the horrible, old uniformed gardeners would appear, waving a big stick and shouting. I never meant any harm, and it always seemed strange that such powerful forces were used to stop little brats like me.

The park was a gateway to the world. All kinds of

people came here, rich and poor. I caught a glimpse into a world beyond the street where I lived. I loved to watch the posh ladies with their fancy clothes from Ballsbridge. They had that confident air of Hollywood actresses who have just received great parts in a movie. To me, they were a different species of women from me ma, me sisters or the girls from my street. They were "real ladies."

Interesting things were always going on in the park, particularly, because it was a haven for lovers. It was the one place you could lie around with a girl and not be sinning. For some reason, in the park, affection in public was okay. Sometimes you'd see a fella lying in the grass kissing a girl. I never knew whether to look or look away. That would distract and fascinate me at the same time, and it made a deep impression on my inner world. But, honest to God, the way they'd eat each other with everyone acting like nothing was happening! Pretending that it was the most normal thing in the world to be snogging passionately, with kids and grannies having their tea all around them. Sometimes, the couple would have the decency to get up and go into the bushes, and you'd hear people saying, "Thank God that trollop isn't my daughter."

I wondered what they meant by that, but I suspected that I saw a little envy on the men's faces. Perhaps, they secretly wanted their daughters to be the one in the bushes. I wondered if that had anything to do with me ma's saying "a bird in the hand is worth two in the bush."

I noticed that the rich people always had an English accent and were Protestant. Maybe that wasn't quite right; I may have made that one up because I didn't know many Protestants. I thought, perhaps God makes those he loves suffer, like us Catholics. Maybe God was an absentee landlord, who had no idea that I was praying to him. This made me sad because if he loved me then how could he spend all this energy on making us all miserable? Why couldn't he spend a second to make our lives a little easier?

The flowerbeds were so beautiful, ordered and structured. They introduced me to the beauty of fragrance and to a world of beauty and order. I felt that I was feeding something inside when I looked at flowers. I wish that I knew then what I know now – that a man's Soul, once reawakened, needs food of the highest order. And that food comes in the form of impressions. I squandered countless hours gazing at those beautiful flowers without understanding how to digest them. Now I know that I was drawn to beauty because my Soul could see beauty, but hadn't grown up enough to know how to feed on it. My Soul didn't know how to exit my body and was relegated, like a doomed prisoner, to observe life through the bars of his cell, watching impotently at the passing world.

I must have got that right because, now, forty years later, I can see each of those moments as if they just occurred. I realize that my clearest memories were filled with joy and sadness, when my Soul must have been watching. That meant that all the other memories occurred when my Soul was asleep or away.

I see now that my childhood was magical and beautiful. When I was sitting in the park, in St. Stephen's Green, God was with me. Sitting on the grass, looking at the Divine arrangement of flowers and the diverse assortment of people in all their craziness, I was observing a replica of the universe. The smells and fragrances represented molecular matter. I imagined that the roses had been like me, blossoming, coming into being, in darkness. Like the roses, unaware of my possibilities, I only saw darkness. But I had actually been germinating, preparing to spring forward into life. How could a rose bush possibly expect the arrival of a rose? Yet one day, it blooms, an explosion of life and color bursting from its dark twig interior. The stem must be staggered by its own beauty. Then an unimaginable, glorious scent emerges – the Soul. Its molecular form rises towards heaven, leaving the earthbound shrub staring agape at its own incomprehensible beauty.

The Soul is enhanced with entirely different properties now. Like an angel, it is free to roam the entire park, free to excite and entice an unassuming passerby with its intoxicating presence. Oh, that one day my Soul too would emerge to freedom, to dance with the garden fairies and angels! The scent of the flowers is the promise of evolution… if I could learn to blossom. Not every rose will flower, and sometimes, after years of solitude and effort, just as one begins to bloom, a young lad will trample it underfoot. I began to suspect that God and his laws were all around us, if we could only see.

Another time in the garden, I saw, in my mind's eye, thousands of abandoned rose and flower Souls dancing in the park. I knew then what fairies were – guides for these newly released flower Souls as they soared to heaven. Perhaps, one day, it will be my role to see human Souls soaring as they are released from the confines of their bodies; perhaps released through death, perhaps through enlightenment, but free, free at last to dance with the nameless one.

The sound of a ringing bell brought me back to reality. But what I had witnessed was far more real and superior to what people called reality. Even at that young age, I knew that not everyone saw what I saw. And not wanting to appear too strange, I kept this to myself. Cherishing these moments in solitude, I knew that one day, like the Ugly Duckling, I would find others like me, and I would experience the scent of each man, woman and child I encountered, as infinitely more intoxicating than fields of roses. Perhaps, I thought, our Souls are the highest essence of all living things to transcend death. I knew I could never see or smell flowers the same way again. And I often practiced my magic at St. Stephen's Green, observing the Souls of flowers.

*

One day, I saw Father Daley and observed how heavy, clumsy and un-flowerlike he was. He was a large, potbellied man with big, ruddy, red cheeks. His teeth were yellow and his eyes were permanently bloodshot. He managed to always smell like booze. I knew that if a man's Soul was near the surface of his body, his energy would be light and childlike. If it did not rely entirely on religious authority, it could float and greet the highest in each man. Father Daley's Soul must have been there somewhere, but buried deep, deep down.

Another day, I saw a young mother shouting full force at her young child who was trying hard to fight back the inevitable tears. That was one of my flower experiencing days so I was very sensitive in that state and I experienced the mother's wrath as if I were her child. I observed that she wasn't there; her Soul had checked out. She wasn't human then. She was like Mrs. Murphy's dog, barking madly in an automatic, preconditioned reaction. I saw shock register on the child's face as he saw an impostor playing the role of his mother. I remember thinking that adults weren't always as sensitive as someone who was experiencing the intoxication of roses. It would be many years of surprising and shocking moments like the one in the park before I would really learn how often people were not present in their own lives, how they abandoned their higher side and left their lower, animal side to claim them.

What an amazing thought: that we might not be here. I knew that my Soul was present when I experienced the roses.

I knew also that there were times when my Soul checked out, because there were huge gaps where I couldn't remember anything. I concluded that there simply must be times when I had gone asleep, like that lady who hurt her child. Reason dictates that she never wanted to hurt her child, and yet parents do. They forget or are taken over by their bodies. Christ! This was giving an entirely new take on the word "possession." Could this mean that our bodies could take over our Souls?

I made the mistake of discussing this with Patsy. I can still remember, to this day, the expression on his face.

"Listen, Fatser," he spat vehemently, "it's as simple as this. You are a fat, fucken' eegit! How can we be taken over by our body when We Are Our Body!"

"But we're not our body!" I protested.

The more I protested, the more I knew I was disturbing something very deep in him, so I gave up and left him in peace.

This was a huge dilemma. So, I asked a beautiful Dominican nun how I could be two things at the same time. She completely confused me by telling me I was, in fact, three, just like the Holy Trinity.

If only she could have explained this to me then and there. God! When I look back on my life, I can pinpoint the moment she could have given me the answer, the answer that could have changed my life. But she didn't. She was either not present or she didn't take my question seriously. Or maybe she just didn't understand what I was asking.

I wouldn't know until much later the true significance of my question. I had to learn the hard way, that first we must learn to ask the questions. That the questions are ultimately more important. Later we can grow into the answers, if that's what we wish. Although I didn't fully understand it, I knew – even when I was two-years-old and had these "rose experiences"—that I was my body and my Soul simultaneously.

IN THE CURTAINS

"Death is a cloak that separates me from the Gods."
--Author unknown

When I was seven-years-old, I developed a severe infection on my left thumb that forced me to stay in bed for several days. As my temperature soared, my parents became quite concerned.

I slept fitfully for most of the day and woke up at twilight. I remember lying there, my head hot against a sweaty pillow, looking at the brown curtains in my bedroom. They were still opened although it was beginning to get dark outside. Suddenly, there was some kind of shift in my perception, a falling, as though I were floating. There was a wonderful feeling of peace and a familiar silence, the silence you feel when there is deep snow on the ground. Then the distance between the curtains and me didn't seem to exist anymore. All I had to do was wish it, and I was right up in the curtains. I "moved" a little further and entered the fabric itself. I could see the molecules in the structure of the fabric. Then molecules themselves parted in my gaze, and I floated beyond, into a void.

Was I in bed or in space? I was neither frightened nor surprised, and a part of me questioned this. Later in my life, this would help me to understand much. It was so incredibly familiar and completely natural for me to exist, see and function as both a telescope and microscope simultaneously. I knew something had happened and now I was disconnected from my body. Here, I was free to move and see things in a way that only angels and the dead could. I remember thinking that I wasn't frightened because I had accepted the fact that I had died. I felt angels near me, but I couldn't see them. Then, I figured that I couldn't be dead since I couldn't see them. Oddly, I wasn't actually thinking these thoughts or feeling relief that I wasn't dead; I was just watching all of it unfold.

I remember realizing that there was no such thing as distance. I saw that only my thoughts and wishes limited me; that I only had to think it and I was there. I saw that distance was a system of measurement for the brain; for my Soul, it was thought. I frolicked in the universe, in my room and in the curtains. I floated around and around, up and down. One moment, I was the universe, and the next, a mere speck. I felt like Alice in Wonderland. This was the way I was supposed to be – always was, and always would be.

Suddenly, I remembered Mervyn. I was full of possibilities and abilities, and yet I didn't know what I was supposed to think or do. Perhaps that's one reason why we're here – to learn to use heaven while we're living in these bodies. I saw my body lying on the bed, the impartial way you'd be aware of your car if you glimpsed it from a window. I was surprised that I was looking at myself with the same indifference that I often found myself looking at other people.

I hoped the sick boy on the bed would get better.

Then came the most puzzling thought of all: If that was me on the bed, then who was the me looking at me? Perhaps it was because I was really caught up in this thought that I lost my beautiful state and snapped back into my body. My body asked "Who am I?" and the other state disappeared, becoming an instant memory. I was suddenly aware of how heavy I was; how slow and primitive even our thoughts are.

I was beginning to suspect that our brains are one of the forces that keep us from being in our Soul. The brain was a big Goliath and the Soul was a little David, but unlike David, I didn't have a slingshot to keep my brain at bay. I couldn't go back to that lovely state no matter how hard I tried. I was now my body and that was that.

*

I still find it amazing that at the age of seven, something in me could associate my experience with a bible story. To this day, when I see Michangelo's David, I am instantly seven-years-old, in my bedroom. I know that the story of David is about the Soul developing something that the body doesn't understand. Goliath didn't know what a slingshot was, nor could he anticipate that it was a potential weapon, and that was David's secret and his advantage. It must be a secret, kept from the body, or the body will disarm it through reason. Perhaps this is what Jesus meant when he advised not to let the left hand know what the right hand is doing. The body, with its ability to question, almost convinced me that I was hallucinating. But to this day, the memory of that beautiful state is very clear. And I know my imagination isn't that good.

Can our Soul and our body really separate? Of course they can. They did then.

If my own body didn't believe me, my mother and father certainly wouldn't and didn't believe me either. It became very clear to me, even at that age, that my Soul was something I was not going to be able to share with other people. If I tried, they would get angry or laugh at me. I believe that every human being has these experiences, experiences that we quickly forget or disregard because they are hard to believe. Maybe it's these moments that flash past us when we die. I wonder how many children with vivid experiences of the Soul have them taken away by their well-meaning parents. A child cries out in the night and then hears, "Sshh, mummy is here." What a tremendous responsibility mothers and fathers take as they ground and guide their children back to humanity.

THE MONK

One night when I was deep in sleep, I suddenly woke up knowing that I was supposed to look at the end of my bed. There in the darkness was a monk in a brown habit with the hood pulled up. He was standing quite still. I couldn't see his face, but I knew he was studying me. We stared at each other for a while.

Once again, I felt no fear, only a great curiosity. Just as I was about to speak, he raised his finger to where his mouth might have been, gesturing for me to be quiet. I understood that he didn't want to disturb my sisters sleeping in the other bed. I was okay with that.

I felt he was going to speak to me as he came around to the side of my bed. I tried very hard to see his face. I remember thinking he was Saint John. I don't know why I had that thought since I'd never heard of Saint John. I felt like a child in the presence of a father whom he adores. Everything was still and peaceful. Again, I felt he was going to speak to me. I was smiling inside; I wanted to reach out and be held by him. I wanted to go home with him because I knew we came from the same place. I think he read my thoughts because he began to move away swiftly, toward the door. I wished he would stay. He must have felt that too, because he turned around and looked slowly at me. I understood then that he couldn't talk to me this time, but that he would be back when the time was right. I knew, too, that he would never be too far away. It was after he went straight through the closed door and vanished that my brain must have kicked in because I could hear myself screaming.

My mother quickly ran into the bedroom followed by my father. My three sisters, awakened by my screams, were now screaming too.

"What in Jesus' name happened?" My mom asked, full of concern, holding me close.

I couldn't talk because my body was so scared. Yet there was a part of me that was taking everything in stride and didn't find anything strange about the monk. Again, here was one side of me studying the other. My mother told me I was only dreaming, but I saw that she wasn't so sure of her words.

My father, meanwhile, went downstairs to check, just in case I had seen a burglar. I knew he didn't believe me either. My older sister, obviously annoyed at being woken up, glowered at me.

"That's what you get for stuffing your face before you go to bed!"

I would often think of my monk. My feelings toward him were always peaceful and loving. I knew that he was looking after me and was never far away. It was many years later, after years of spiritual preparation, that I realized he was indeed the great Spanish mystic, Saint John of the Cross.

***

STUDENT STORY: WILLIAM

I was 25 years old when I met Mervyn Brady. It was late summer, 1992. I first said hello to him in a hotel in London's Notting Hill district. He was spending the evening with a well-known musician/ pop star, a former Academy student who was a mutual friend (at that time I worked as a manager in marketing at Sony Music). An hour and a half later, we emerged from a stretch limousine at a nightclub in Richmond, another affluent suburb of London. The nightclub was called Apollo or something and the inside was all metal grids and Perspex plastic and brushed aluminum. It was supposed to resemble the inside of a spaceship.

For years after, Mervyn would chuckle when he'd introduce me to new students and say in his soft Dublin accent," I met William in a forkin' spaceship."

Also present in the nightclub were many celebrities, and while most of our party got down to drinking and dancing, I found myself standing next to Mervyn Brady. A guy as skinny as a rake (me) and a guy weighing nearly thirty stone. We looked a picture. It was there that we had our first conversation. The music was unbelievably loud and we shouted ear-to-ear to make ourselves heard.

That conversation changed my life forever. It went something like this:

William: So Mervyn, what do you do then?

Mervyn: I'm a Philosopher.

W: And you're mates with Darrien, right?

M: Yes. I teach him. He's one of my students.

W: So you teach?

M: Yes. I have a school in Los Angeles and a school here in London.

W: So what exactly do you teach?

M: At our Academy we teach Awakening.

W: Awakening?

M: What do you think about life, William? Do you think there's more to it?

W: Oh definitely. I mean I have this cool job and everything but I see through it, the glamour and that. Sometimes I feel that there has to be more to it (life). In fact, I've always felt like this, but life has its distractions, you know. Lately, I've been reading a lot of books about the Soul. Is that like Awakening?

M: Very much so. It seems that you're asking the right sort of questions. Would you like to ask one now?

W: Okay. Is there anything that I can do that will help me? I mean I have this great job and I can't just leave it. In fact I don't want to. But I want to get in touch with my Soul.

M: William, that's a perfect question. I'm going to tell you a secret. When you're next in a nightclub like this, or at a gig, or just at a party with your mates, just remember that you're here.

W: I don't get you…

M: *Remember to be in the moment. It's like 'I'm here in this nightclub, talking to William.' I remember I am. I observe the moment.*

W: *Right. Okay. I get that. And that will help me, will it?*

M: *It's a big secret, William. Now you know it. And now you can make use of it.*

W: *Okay, I'll try it. Thanks.*

The rest of the evening was spent going from one nightclub to the next, surrounded by the nightlife of London in a stretched Daimler limousine. Pop stars, drink, babes, Big Irish Philosophers... as first impressions go, this was quite a big one.

We chatted some more that night, Mervyn and I, over a few vodkas. And when we reached the final club of the night, I remember going upstairs to a VIP area where Mervyn was sitting with Darrien and some babes. Around 2.30 a.m. Mervyn saw me and got up from the table, using his stick; it was a considerable effort as he was at his heaviest at that time. He walked over to me and asked how I was.

"Oright, Wil?" (Sometimes he used to adopt a mock cockney accent.)

"Yeah, sure."

"Now, you're here," Mervyn said. "Remember to be here."

"I already am," I said. "I can't stop. I've been doing it since you said it three hours ago."

Mervyn laughed, smiled, and asked me if I'd like his phone number. I punched it into my mobile phone and said I'd get in touch. It was almost a year later when I did so. Although the next time we'd meet, it would be a considerably different meeting.

*

Almost a year had passed since I first met Mervyn in the spaceship. And, like he had suggested, I had been "remembering myself" for much of that time. I didn't know what I was doing, really, but it was a process that seemed to be gaining momentum.

My friends and I—all of us were in our mid-twenties— decided to start a group. The group's aim was to meet once a week very early in the morning, around 6 a.m. We all had different ideas as to what our intention was. Some of us felt that the group was an opportunity to expand our ideas. Two members decided that they wanted to become super successful in life. They had been reading Anthony Robbins' self-empowerment books with titles like, "Be A Millionaire in the Next Two Years!" That kind of stuff. For myself, I just wanted to feel right.

After a few weeks, the meetings with my friends were creating results and we all enjoyed them very much. I had started reading books on meditation and inner peace. And after the meetings I would meditate for maybe an hour in my bedroom. Then I would go to work. Through the books I was reading, which were mainly eastern in their philosophy, I had picked up on the idea of "walking without crutches." I decided to give up everything that I felt I was using as a crutch – simple things, like coffee, smoking marijuana, and watching TV.

I was getting up at 5 a.m. for our 6 a.m. meetings and meditation. One Sunday morning I awoke early and spent a couple of hours meditating. A feeling began to build inside me and, suddenly, I felt elated and needed to go to the park at the top of the road. I stood in the park, looked at the trees and began to cry. I wasn't really sure why I was crying, but it was like I could see. The trees where there as always, but I could see them. I stayed in the park, feeling like something beautiful was happening to me. I knew that it must in some way have been the product of the efforts of self remembering I had been making. But this emotion was all consuming and I had no idea where it was coming from.

I spoke to a friend from work, Eve, and explained to her how different I was feeling. I told her about the group and the books and the energy, and she suggested that I ring Mervyn. She'd been spending time with Darrien, as her job was international TV promotions and during the last few months she had met Mervyn a few times socially since he had been with Darrien in the US and in the UK. She had been impressed that Mervyn was a philosopher and, sensing my energy and excitement, I suppose she felt it natural that we meet up.

A couple of weeks later, Eve had arranged for Mervyn and me to meet for lunch in a small Italian restaurant in London's Soho district.

"So...William," began Mervyn. "Nice to see you again. Last time I saw you, we were in the spaceship in Richmond. It's been a while – how have you been?"

"I wanted to talk with you," I said, "because Eve said you may be able to help me understand all these things that I've been experiencing."

"What do you mean?"

"Well, I started doing that self-remembering thing that you told me about. And I've been doing it since I last saw you."

I explained to Mervyn about the group, the early morning meetings, the meditation, and giving up the coffee, and the experience in the park.

He looked and me and laughed. "Wow!"

"What're you laughing at?"

"Oh no, William, not you," he said. "It's just that I have a group of students – did I tell you I was a teacher? And if I suggested that they get up at five in the morning for a meeting, well, they'd probably tell me to fook off!" He carried on laughing.

We ordered some food; I think Mervyn had a grilled chicken and caesar salad and I remember he took some mayonnaise with tip of his knife and tasted it. Then he looked at me and asked me to describe my life, my desires, my passions. At this point, I had no idea why he was so interested in me. But in retrospect, I can see that he was gauging my body type, feature, center of gravity, friction. He was assessing my mechanics.

"I think I've found the path, Mervyn," I declared.

"William," he said, "you may have found the path, but now you have a mountain to climb."

I was a little deflated. Not a mountain. Please.

He mentioned the story of Snow White and told me that it was written by esoteric schools to describe the process of what was happening to me.

"Which is what?"

"You're beginning to awaken," he said.

"Awaken?"

"There are different energies that the machine can generate," he explained. "The body can go as high as say 12 or 6; these are just terms. I'll describe them in detail later. The soul uses an energy similar to 12. The energies that you have been experiencing belong to your soul. You are beginning to awaken, William. Your soul is literally waking up."

I was speechless. On one hand everything felt right and yet it all seemed so surreal. I really had no idea what all of this meant.

"What else can you tell me?" I asked him, keen to know more.

"That your body type is Solar," he said. "And that you're probably emotionally centered*."

"And you can tell all this just by being with me? I mean I have no idea what this means. What is Solar? What is emotionally centered**? And what do you mean by different energies?"

"Well, Solar is a way of classifying your machine. Emotionally centered is how some people use their brain, and as for different energies…" Mervyn paused, then he held his left hand a few inches above the table. "This is forty-eight, the energy of your everyday life. And this is twelve," he said, lifting his hand much higher, "a lighter state, like when you're in love."

He looked directly at me and smiled, but said nothing further. All I felt was excitement. I knew that I had met a great new friend, although I had no idea what or where this lunch meeting would lead to. This system of classifying energy was something I hadn't come

---

*'Solar' and 'emotionally centered' are terms from an esoteric system, used as tools, to help understand ourselves, others and our relationships.

across before in any of the books that I'd been reading. Mervyn had hinted that Fairy Tales and Awakening was part of a much larger system but had expanded no further, other than he was a teacher and had students in Los Angeles and London.

Mervyn told me that he was going to LA the following day for a month to six weeks. He asked if I would mind if he told his students about our lunch meeting and what I had told him about my friends' group and my experiences with self-remembering and the energy that I didn't understand. He said he'd call me when he got back and maybe we could meet for lunch again? Definitely, I told him. But I was still a little confused as I said my goodbye.

I was keen to know more so that afternoon after work I ran to a new age book store nearby and bought about three or four books with the word "soul" in the title. I literally devoured those books, one after the other. I had an insatiable appetite for this new experience, and now I had a name for it too: Awakening. My new friend had gone to LA and I was incredibly happy. Everything seemed possible. I even had a new girlfriend. I'd met her at Top of the Pops (a TV show with music and live performers) where she had come to see Darrien. I had been incredibly low for the previous six months and now I was incredibly high. Life now seemed very different; from now on everything would go my way. I was so sure.

A Letter from William to a New Student

Dear Olivia,

Your articulation of what is happening to your inner world reminded me of my own experiences when I joined this work.

About seven years ago I was also hit with massive doses of incredible energy. Like lightning in a thunderstorm, seemingly out of nowhere, the energy had struck and pierced a burning hole so vast in my delicate armor that I knew I would never be the same.

Thinking that I was going mad and acutely aware that I wasn't at all in control of the state that I was in, I considered psychiatric help. In desperation, I remembered the man I had met for the first time, a year earlier, in a nightclub resembling a spaceship. He was a philosopher whose life's work was dedicated to the rooting out and growing of souls amongst men and women. I'd met him again a few months prior to this over lunch and he'd pointed me in the direction of a few books, but he certainly didn't seem like a psychiatrist. I wasn't sure, but I thought that maybe this man could help me?

After a few frantic phone calls to the States, we arranged to meet at his house in South East London on his return.

Once a posturing, over-confident, South London boy, I sat before him now, reduced to tears. I had been crying almost continually for seven days and my machine was in bits.

"What is happening to me?" were the only words that came out.

Mervyn smiled, and in an instant I began to feel at peace.

We talked for hours, about the school, the quest for God, and

51

the road ahead.

I left this warm, big bear of a man around midnight. What little strength I had left took me the short walk up the garden path to my car. Stopping briefly to look at the stars, I was overwhelmed by the enormity of the feelings that overcame me. I had never, ever felt so small. I only knew that my future was somehow connected to this man that I had only met twice before.

The next few weeks were very difficult. At work I felt I could no longer do my job. I had this feeling of being so fragile, and yet there was still this tremendous energy pervading my being, a peace that I had craved for as long as I could remember.

I awoke one morning with a feeling of ecstasy and realization and called Mervyn.

"Mervyn...." the words stuttered out, "am I an angel?"

Mervyn paused and then said, "Of sorts. Come along to the meeting tonight and I'll expand further."

I remember my first meeting as if it was yesterday. I picked Mervyn up from his house and we arrived at the Academy flat. I think, bar one, all the students there that night are still with the Academy. We walked across Blackheath to the front door and Mervyn pointed to the moon and my first lecture had begun.

My first sense, as I was introduced to the group, was one of sincere familiarity. Over the coming weeks I confided to the group that, as certain as I was that I had somehow found my life's true work (or it had found me), I could not help feeling so fragile and naked.

"You need to grow roots," Mervyn told me. And he was right.

The Academy is so important because it can give us the tools with which we can go back into life. It can help us acquire a suit of armor that will protect our most precious cargo, while at the same time allowing nurturing and growth. For a period, I had never felt so vulnerable and alone, and now I had true friends – others who were walking the same path as I was. I knew that I would never be alone again.

A true school can be distinguished by the fruits of its teachings. The miraculous first happened to me seven years ago. The Academy has enabled me to connect with the miraculous many times since. I now have my roots and have learned how to survive in life. In my garden a wisteria vine was planted four summers ago. During the first summer there were no flowers, the second summer a few bloomed, the third summer a few more flowers bloomed, but this year, there are literally hundreds. Nature is a constant reminder to me of how higher forces work. Summer sun is the miraculous energy that enabled the vine to blossom.

This year I was taken aback at the beauty and solidity of the vine. It had grown its roots deep enough to reach the most fertile of soil and the miraculous sunlight had given birth to hundreds of these delicate flowers.

Welcome to all the new students that I have not yet met; be assured that there are others like you. The Academy vine may have its roots in many different countries, but its scent has the power of diffusion and can mingle on the wind.

A Warm Heart,
William

4

A WORLD ON A BUS

A beginner in this work means someone who has begun. It means that they have begun again where they left off the last time.

For each student this is a very different starting point. For one, the starting point may be at a much different place than another student who is meeting the work for the first time. This is one reason why longevity in this work is not an accurate picture of where one stands in relation to it.

Every angle is important, as we do not always know, or can judge from how deep within one it came from.

Some of the most refreshing angles I have heard are from people right at the beginning of their re-entry.

--Excerpt from "A Beginner in the Work"
 Meeting, January 2000

THE LAMP POST

One of the best things about getting on a bus is that once you're on one, you're going somewhere. My friends and I took the #79 bus to O'Connell St. Bridge, and there the world opened up. Most of the time, we just played on our road or went to the park, but the bus took us to another world.

Getting off the bus was an art. We would all line up on the platform of the double-decker, and as it was coming into the stop, we'd hold the rail and jump off. You had to lean back and start running the moment your feet hit the ground or you'd fall forward onto your face. Harry explained that it was the wind that kept you up when you were leaning back and running.

We loved watching old fellas jump off too soon. They would start running as they jumped off and because their legs weren't able to move fast enough, they'd fall forward, legs flailing, on their faces. This was a kind of rite of passage: when you fell on your face once or twice, it told everyone that you were an old fart. In fact, in hindsight, there were a lot of old fellas in Dublin with scabs on their faces.

Once Eamon Early jumped off when the bus was going real fast. I'll always remember the look on his face as he saw the lamp post in front of him, but the wind was too strong for him to stop, and he had no choice but to smash into it. He was knocked out and moaning on the ground. The bus stopped. The conductor and all the old ones ran out yelling and swearing at him. It always amazed me how adults loved to find new ways to tell you off. We learned a lot of great new expressions.

Eamon was our hero for a while. We loved to sit around as he told us all the amazing things that went through his head while he saw the lamp post coming. We could never figure out how he had so much time to think or see all those things in only a couple of seconds. Jesus, he even told us he saw his dead grandmother and heard her calling him. Harry told us the lamp post damaged his brain.

I couldn't help but believe Eamon a little bit. He assured me that he ran, slow motion, into the lamp post. Something in me recognized what he was saying, but I wasn't going to argue with Harry. So, I gave in to peer pressure and agreed with the guys that Eamon was nuts, even though I knew he wasn't. I felt nuts for believing two conflicting things at the same time. How can you see opposite things and not know which one was right?

GIRLS AND THE LOVE STUFF

At the bus queue, you'd often hear the older women discussing their operations or someone who died and how they died. You learned all sorts of things here. The bus queue could be a very harrowing experience.

The buses didn't always run on time, and in the morning rush hour they were usually full by the time they reached our road. The conductor would only let one or two people on and ring the bell four times, which would signal the driver not to stop for any more fares. Then everybody would unite in a chorus of curses and complaints. Isn't it funny how a little bit of negativity brings people together? Maybe that's how wars begin.

Anyway, I'd always go upstairs when I got on the bus. If I was lucky, a girl in a miniskirt would be in front of me, and I could get a good eyeful. Some girls never even noticed. They were always the prettiest ones and seemed so nice to talk to that you'd feel guilty for looking up their skirts. Maybe I learned guilt, too, on the #79 bus.

Sometimes you'd look up by mistake, and catch a glimpse of an old one's legs: nylons hanging off of varicose veined legs wearing those great big "belly warmer" knickers. You'd try to look away real fast, but, too late, the impression had gone into you: instant pain in your crotch. They were the kind of old women who insisted on kissing you at parties, red lipstick, smelling of spirits. They always smelled like

Johnson's Baby Powder; you just knew they shook it down their knickers.

One day, after a lot of pushing and shoving, I looked up, and a beautiful girl, who I still can see in my mind's eye to this day, walked up the stairs in front of me. She had on a short, white skirt and a pair of those American knickers, the real small ones that go up your arse. She looked down and caught me having a good look. I froze, anticipating a lecture, but instead she gave me the most beautiful smile I had ever seen.

I looked behind me and saw that four fellas, coming up the stairs, had caught her beautiful smile and her lovely American knickers. We looked at each other, stunned. We exchanged glances and smiled like we had just won the lottery.

I'd never witnessed anything like this before, and from that moment on I understood something about God and love. I experienced a surge of energy that was Divine, not dirty. Sometimes when you think dirty thoughts, you know that they are wrong. But the beauty of this smiling girl was so pure and lovely, it made me and the fellas feel great for the rest of the day. I thought that if all doctors employed girls like her you'd forget you were sick.

THE SECRET OF SMILING

In the winter we stood in the snow, and when you made eye contact with someone, you'd say something stupid like, "Cold, isn't it?" and shuffle from foot to foot. I spent a lot of time looking at the ground. Everybody did. If you caught someone's eye, they might start talking to you. There was a certain type that would stare hard at me, and that would make me stare even harder at the ground because I knew what was coming.

"Why don't you go on a diet? I mean look at the fat fucken' state of you! For God's sake!"

"Leave him alone and mind your own business!"

There was always someone who would defend me, and most of the time I didn't even know them.

Anyway, that's why I have such a good memory of what people wore on their feet. I used to think some women had no feeling in their feet – the little high heels they wore in the freezing snow. They had huge coats and nearly bare feet.

At the bus stop I learned a great secret that still applies today. If you stare at someone, hoping to attract their attention, and they suddenly look at you, what do you think they're going to see? You. Staring at them. Now, that can be very offensive or frightening. So you have to pay attention. When they look at you, SMILE, and most of the time they will smile back. But if it's a nice girl, you have to clear your head of all dirty thoughts or they'd know, and scowl at you.

If you put an "experiencing the roses" look on your face, you are guaranteed a smile.

Harry told me that I looked real stupid when I did that.

"They're only feeling sorry for you, Fatser. They think you're a poor unfortunate."

And with that he nearly killed all my joy of smiling at girls.

*

When it rained and you had an umbrella, you hoped a girl would come by so you could offer to share yours. But girls are far cleverer than men; they nearly always had one. Then the guys standing in the rain would look at you as if you were a pansy or a mammy's boy. There used to be a big macho thing in Dublin about taking the rain. "Scared of a drop of rain are ya', Fatser?" or "Sure, a drop of rain never killed anyone." If you were too well wrapped up that was grounds for abuse too. Harry would take off his jacket in the rain and put it in his school bag. "To keep the shagging thing dry," he explained.

COWBOYS AND INDIANS

When we were about seven or eight, we played cowboys and Indians. We didn't have the right toys, so we improvised. Harry got the great idea to empty a tin can and grab a stick and took us all to the bus stop. We were buzzing with excitement because Harry always had the best ideas. We waited at the bus stop, wondering, as Harry put the stick in the can and set it on the street. We stood around watching the can and stick, not knowing what to expect, but anticipating something good.

The bus came by and flattened the tin can onto the stick – a tomahawk! Harry Kennedy had reinvented the tomahawk! Harry was a genius! Soon everyone had one, and if they broke, all you had to do was go to the bus stop to make another one. This was all fine until one day it resulted in a great tragedy.

Derek Morris was a big dope, and you always had to look out for him. He went to the bus stop and set his tin can and stick on the street, fine. But the stupid dope sat on the curb, sticking out his two legs with the tomahawk between his feet. The bus took a long time, and he apparently forgot where his feet were, because the bus ran over his legs.

He didn't say anything. He just sat there with his jaw open like he had seen a ghost. Thank God, the hospital was able to fix him up.

Our parents banned us from making tomahawks, and

from then on another of Harry's brilliant inventions slipped into oblivion.

THE BLUE LADY

Another day I was standing at the bus stop with my mother and big sister. Suddenly, Madeleine ran in front of the bus, and in slow motion I saw it swallow her up. My mother was screaming, the bus tires were screeching, and all hell broke loose.

I remember thinking that I didn't want to see my sister all squashed up, and I seemed to have the time to try to figure out why she did that. The driver and conductor ran to my hysterical mother. Then the driver became hysterical and everyone at the bus stop started screaming. Passengers poured off the bus screaming. Soon there were fifty or sixty people screaming.

Nobody knew what to do. Should they move the bus or get a crane to remove her? But for some reason I was strangely calm. I looked down at the front of the bus, and I wasn't surprised to see my sister's hand reaching from under the bus as she began to crawl out. I remember thinking that my mother would be so angry, because there was oil and grease all over her school uniform.

"Sweet Jesus, Mary and Joseph! She's alive!"

Then everybody started screaming again. Me mother ran over to help her to her feet. Suddenly, it was like something gave everyone permission to release and the bus driver fainted and everybody else started yelling at my sister for nearly killing everyone on the bus. By now a huge crowd had gathered, and one of the local priests, Father Murphy, was talking to my sister.

They were all dumbstruck when my sister kept saying, "The Lady in Blue showed me the way out from under the bus." Father Murphy and my mother kept exchanging strange glances, not daring to say what they were thinking. For me it was very simple: the Virgin Mary appeared and helped my sister out. The Virgin Mary decided it wasn't Madeleine's day to die. But Father Murphy told my mother that Madeleine was hallucinating and advised that we keep quiet about the Blue Lady.

When we got home, I asked my sister to tell me what really happened. She told me that she didn't know how to get out from under the bus, and the Blue Lady took her by the hand and led her out. When the Lady appeared, everything went quiet and moved in slow motion. Madeleine said the Lady in Blue was the most serene and beautiful thing she had ever seen.

Father Murphy had been within six feet of an entire lifetime of prayers and devotions, and I noted then that he really missed the boat.

MRS. O'CONNOR, THE FIGHTING IRISH

Another day, when the bus arrived, the conductor only let on five people. "Five only, standing inside," he ordered. But the passengers weren't going to put up with that and started pouring onto the bus.

The conductor, a little red-haired fella who looked like a poor Woody Allen, tried in vain to stop the rush. When he saw that no more passengers could even stand on the platform, he shouted, "No more! Full up!"

As the bus slowly moved off, I saw Mrs. O'Connor falling off the bus, still clutching her handbag. The bus screeched to a stop. I believe I saw in miniature the spirit of "The fighting Irish." She pulled herself to her feet and charged at the bus. She pulled the first fella off and whacked him over the head with her handbag. Kicking and screaming, she bashed everyone standing on the platform and sent them all flying. Then, she charged "Woody Allen" who was cowering in the bus, dragged him out onto the street and boxed his ears. "Ya' little bastard, you nearly killed me!" If it wasn't for the driver running around from his cab, she might have killed him. Then she got onto the bus like nothing had happened, and off went the bus, leaving behind all the people she threw off. We all agreed that she was totally mad and should be locked up at the Grange Gorman Asylum.

Another day, while we were waiting again at that same

bus stop, we heard shouting coming out of a nearby house. The front door crashed open, and we heard, "Piss outside, ya' scrawny bastard!" Then we saw this black thing flying through the air. It was only when it hit the ground and ran off that we realized it was a cat. Startled, we started cracking up.

Harry told us it was okay because cats have special bones that you can't break. He promised to give us a demonstration one day.

SCUTTIN'

In today's society, scuttin' would be almost impossible because everything moves so fast. In Dublin, nothing moved that fast and some mad young fellas would even scut on the bus. Scuttin' meant that you took a free ride on a moving vehicle without the driver knowing. So we'd all stand at the bus stop and get on real slow while Harry and a few other fellas went around the back of the bus and climbed onto the bumper, holding on to the rear lights. It never was too far to the next stop on the way to school, so they didn't have to hang on for long.

We knew you shouldn't scut on a town bound bus because they go superfast on the main road. This, of course, left you exposed to being caught by a garda car, which meant you'd get a good hiding from them, and then they'd haul you back to your family. After your parents got over the initial shock of finding the police at your house, you'd get another hiding.

Anyway, I remember one day Harry was scuttin', and when we got on at the first stop the conductor asked him if he was getting on or not. Harry replied that he wasn't. When we reached the next stop, sure enough, there was Harry again. After Harry kept appearing after six stops, the conductor asked, "are you a fucken' magician or what?" At the seventh stop, Harry got on the bus, bold as brass, and only had to pay half the fare because he was already half way there.

Sometimes if we were lucky, the bread man would pass the bus stop with his horse and van. That was the best. Even I could scut on that. We'd pass the next bus stop, very slowly, and watch the passengers' expressions as the van passed with seven or eight of us kids hanging on the back.

Sometimes we had to kick off other kids who wanted to get on. One day, I told Harry I was sorry for the poor horse that had to pull all that extra weight up the hill. Harry explained that it was no problem for a horse; all it meant was that the horse could breathe better. We saw that this was true – we did see more steam coming out of the horse's mouth when he was pulling you.

Scuttin' on the milkman's cart was almost impossible. He hired a kid on each road to guard his milk because he knew it wouldn't last two minutes when he went to a house to make his delivery. He did this a lot. And we soon figured out where he would go in to "wet his whistle."

Harry told us the milkman was father to half the kids on the street, but this time we didn't believe him because we all had daddies.

* * *

STUDENT STORY: NADIA
EMAIL TO ACADEMY, JANUARY 2000

Dear All,

This morning Mervyn and I had breakfast in Ramsgate, in his favourite restaurant called the "Four Seasons." It is his favourite because it appears it is the best of a bad lot. He often talks of a super place he goes to in Hollywood called Norm's. It is the only time I see him becoming close to what appears to be identified*, as he talks of the copious amounts of coffee one can drink there for a mere dollar. I know that when I go to L.A. I wish to dine at this landmark.

He looked excited despite the rain and the cold, and he quickly ordered two steaming mugs of tea. "I know who I am," he said excitedly. "My Higher centers told me this morning."

Now he had my full, undivided attention and he told me the following fascinating story:

---

* *'Identified' is a Fourth Way term that means to be consumed by a thought, feeling or sensation. If we honestly observe ourselves in identification, we find that in this state we are no longer a human being entertaining an idea. We become that thought, feeling or sensation, helpless and held captive by it.*

"I was asleep in first state this morning and I saw myself on a familiar hill, talking to a crowd of people. I had their attention and my Higher Centers wafted out all over the people. Then I heard myself saying, 'I HAVE COME TO...'

"At this point my machine leapt with interest; it was finally going to find out who or what I was, and it woke me up into second state as I heard the end of the sentence. 'I HAVE COME TO REMIND YOU. I AM THE REMINDER.'"

He looked at me and was beaming. I was a little puzzled and asked him what he meant. He said, "First, to remind you of who you really are, and not who your machine thinks it is. You have forgotten who you are, Nadia."

I looked into his eyes and was transported into a delicious higher state, and I smiled at him as a child would at an adored father.

He was right. I do forget who or what I am and spend most of my life in negativity and imagination. I forget the beautiful Soul that I am and the beauty that I am capable of beholding. I realized then that he was my re-minder, that he re-minded me from the machine I was becoming and gave me back my real mind, my Soul.

"You see Nadia," Mervyn said, "I am the reminder. Henceforth I will devote the rest of my life to re-minding. Let us remind people of who they are. Jesus gave people an identity. They were 'Sons and Daughters of God' and they have forgotten. All we have to

do is re-mind them. William Blake was The Interpreter. I am The Reminder."

It was obvious Mervyn was seeing into another world, and he said, "If someone minds you and you run away or get lost like a sheep, a New Shepherd finds you and he will be your re-minder. In other words, he will re-mind you. So I will re-mind and re-mind and I will be The Reminder."

He spoke very quickly about how the Academy would set about this New Triad of Reminding. He seemed to understand what he was saying, and I think I heard him "Thanking God" for this new role.

Breakfast was served by a young lady, and he smiled at her. Then he said, "I just re-minded her."

My mind was racing with thoughts and feelings. I felt I knew what he was talking about, yet there seemed so much to digest. Somehow I knew I had been alone in this world, with only my flesh and blood parents to mind me, but now I felt reminded of the deeper, real me.

We left the restaurant and he asked me to tell you all about the revelation. I forgot until tonight. But I am sure something or someone somewhere reminded me.

Love,
Nadia

* * *

5
UNDERSTANDING GOD

I am convinced that one of the major reasons we are here is for the Soul and therefore for the Gods to see, feel and hear and experience creation in all its forms through us.

I know how much I have learned by watching a negative student or watching a student struggling just as I did and still do with myself.

So whatever your machine is doing, share it with the Soul. It will not judge you. It only wants to learn. If you are painting a room or kissing a girl, let the Soul in on it.

That is the Work. The triad (sacred aim) is wrong if one thinks there have to be certain conditions to start Self-Remembering.

--Excerpt from "Forgiveness and Grace"
 Online meeting, August 2000

THE SCAMS

"My sleeping friends are so unkind.
How easily they change their minds about love and friendship."
--Author unknown

Whenever our parents bought lemonade, we would fight over who would bring back the empty bottles. This was because Delany's, the local shop, would give you a penny or an ice cream for each bottle. It wasn't unusual to see kids going along the street with a big bag of empty bottles to exchange them for goodies. But more likely than not, they would have a note from their mother asking for bread or butter, real food, in exchange.

But when a kid could get away with it, you'd see him asking for two ounces of butter and a quarter pound of sugar. Usually the fathers would get butter and the kids would get margarine. Of course, that was in the poor houses. My mother was always proud of the fact that we had good food on the table, and that we had butter. The cult of butter was amazing. Families were secretly judged for being margarine users, and you would make excuses for not going to a fella's house, knowing you would only get margarine.

I remember how Harry was so proud of me when I told him of an inspiration from God that I had one night about Delany's shop. Or maybe it was from the devil.

The next day we snuck around the back of the shop,

and just as my inspiration had foreseen, there was a load of crates – full of empty bottles. They were all nicely stacked up for the deliveryman to collect later in the day. There was no one around and we took three bottles each from two different cases at the bottom of the pile and then walked around to the front of the shop to sell them back to Mr. Delany. We swore we wouldn't tell a Soul, and this kept us in sweets and ice cream for a long time. I had my first taste of what it was like to be really rich.

Of course you can't keep something like this a secret for very long, and we ended up telling Eamon Early. Some people aren't cut out to be great criminals like Harry and me, that's for sure. The stupid "eegit" went around to the back of the shop, stole a whole crate and brought it around to the front. Mr. Delaney gave him a clatter around the ears, threatened to ring the garda and tell his old man.

The next day there was a fence around the bottles and the good life was over for Harry and me. I didn't feel too bad about our lemonade bottle scam because Harry said it was only a venial sin and not a "mortaler." A "mortaler" you could go to hell for.

"Lemonade bottles aren't alive. That's why it's only venial," Harry explained knowingly.

We used to have great discussions about what was a "mortaler." Sure, we knew that we weren't supposed to kill anyone or take God's name in vain, but that wasn't what interested us. We wanted to know about real mortal sin.

Patsy Whealan told us that he heard if you kiss a girl for more than two seconds it was a "mortaler." This threw us into all kinds of imagination and the start of a heated discussion. Harry, as usual, stole the show by pointing out that if a girl sees your cock you go straight to hell, no questions asked.

"Then what happens if you shit in front of a girl?" asked Derek Shannon. He was always trying to trap Harry.

We were all dumbfounded by the question. We stared at Harry.

"Don't be so fucken' stupid!" Harry responded by giving Derek a clatter around the ear.

"Well, my sister and her husband shit in front of each other!" Derek retorted.

Now he had our full attention. We looked at each other in amazement, trying to conjure up the image, our noses slowly wrinkling in horror or delight or something.

"It's not a sin if you're married," Harry answered evenly, "only if you're just going out with someone."

We all burst out laughing, probably in collective relief of not having to shit in front of a girl for a long time.

"I guess a mortaler is anything disgusting or anything that makes you feel disgusted," concluded Con Scott.

Then Pierce O'Connor, the quiet one among us, spoke. "A mortaler is when some of our fathers," he wisely didn't mention any names, "come home on Friday nights, pissed as Lords, puking in the middle of the road or in somebody's garden. That's a mortaler that the good book don't talk about."

It's funny the way we all looked at Harry. We all knew he was talking about his da, and so did Harry. I think that was the first time I ever saw him worried.

I loved these discussions - when we would all sit around and share our knowledge and experiences. Secretly I wanted to know all about sin – in order to understand it. I mean, imagine doing something for years that you thought was normal and then one day discovering it was a sin? God had left us a tricky path if you wanted to be good.

Patsy Whealen told us that he heard his older sister talking about "the deadly sins." Apparently they were the real baddies.

"Like what?" We asked in fascination at this horrible new discovery.

"Like gluttony."

My heart sank as they all stared at me. I felt the devil coming for me.

"I'm naturally fat," I said quietly. Although I was too young to know the word "suicidal," I felt it. I was terrified. My worst nightmare had been realized. And it was Harry who saved me.

"Don't you know that kids can't commit deadly sin? And it's a deadly sin only after you turn twelve and make your confirmation," Harry explained slowly.

I sighed in relief that I could be fat for another four

years.

"Fatser is still alive, isn't he? I mean, if he was committing a deadly sin all the time he'd be dead by now. Right?" Harry concluded victoriously.

They all nodded in solemn agreement.

Then someone asked Patsy if he knew of any other deadly sins and he said he heard something about "sloth."

"What the fuck does an Australian bear got to do with this?" smirked Derek.

Harry informed him that it was only a deadly sin if you killed one.

The confusing thing about sin is that I really wanted to be good, but sometimes it was just so easy to be bad. I remember one day opening my mother's purse when she was out. I planned to take a sixpence for an ice cream.

"That's stealing," boomed this big voice in my head.

For a second I thought it was God himself speaking. Then I recognized the voice; it was my mum's voice in my head. I reasoned that since she wasn't home, I could ignore the voice and started to take the money.

"You're committing a sin," warned the next voice. This voice I knew wasn't my mum's but my guardian angel's. Don't ask me how I knew this, I just did. So I grabbed the money real fast and ran for the door. I tried to never think about it again. Perhaps we go to sleep or forget things or forget ourselves. Perhaps when we are young we need God, our guardian angel, the priests, the schoolteachers and our mothers to watch us, yet we still sin. It just shows how strong the devil or that something bad in me really is.

Who in their wildest dreams would believe that forty years later, fellas we never heard of called psychologists would be saying that we should let the child figure out what is right and respect the child's moral compass. Jesus! In Dublin, in the fifties, without my group of elders looking after me, I would have been a sitting duck for the devil. Kids have to be taught the ways of the society they are born into; reliance on their inner voice is futile, no matter how holy it is.

FIRST CONFESSION

All fifty of my classmates were marched in pairs up to the church to make our first confession, half to the right box, and the other half to the left box. I remember being so worried that I would forget this procedure that I hardly noticed it was my turn to go in.

Then Brother Coleman tapped me on the shoulder, and I took a giant step into the unknown. Now I had to face God and He knew everything. No holding back and no lying. The door opened. There I was, alone in a big black box, like a coffin, and I knew God and all his holy angels were waiting to hear me confess. Suddenly, a hole in the wall covered by a grille opened up, and right in front of my face was the one human being who terrified me more than anyone else on earth – Father Daley himself.

He muttered some secret words in Latin and asked me to begin my confession.

"Forgive me Father for I have sinned. This is my first confession." And at that moment I couldn't remember any of my sins and became tongue-tied.

"Well, have you sinned?" he asked.

It was as if God himself was asking and I knew I must have sinned.

"Yes Father, I told lies, I didn't do what my mother and father told me and I had dirty thoughts," I confessed in panic.

Jesus Christ! To this day, I can't figure out why I said

that. I later reasoned that it was all I could think of in the moment. Funny how there are moments in your life when you watch events unfolding, and you have absolutely no power to intervene in any way. You know what's going to happen next, and it does.

"Exactly what kind of dirty thoughts did you have?" he asked.

"I thought of going to the toilet in front of a girl." It was the only mortaler I could think of in that moment.

"You mean a number one or two?"

I didn't know what this meant so I took a guess and said, "A number two."

Father Daley was really quiet for long time.

"I absolve you from your sins." And I think he said, "May God forgive you."

He told me to say three Hail Mary's, three Our Father's and three Glory Be to the Father's for my penance. I was sure he peeked out from the curtain to see who I was as I went back to the penance bench.

I was so embarrassed. I hoped God would understand that I just made it up.

Then that voice in my head said, "It's the fucken' truth, you did think it." I cringed but I couldn't really swear that I didn't think it, so I prayed really hard asking God to forgive me, just in case. I saw the other fellows with their heads really bowed. They seemed so sincere that I wondered who taught them to pray like that. Nobody ever showed me. I wanted to pray with my whole being, but I didn't know how so I bent down really as far as I could and begged God to forgive me because I was so bad. Then suddenly, I felt it was ridiculous to be asking for forgiveness when I didn't really do anything wrong. I distinctly remember that there was another me looking at the me that was pretending to pray really hard. It's hard to describe, it was such a beautiful, mystical experience.

I think it was my Soul. It didn't think or judge, it just looked and seemed to record everything that was going on. It was a familiar feeling: a silence and a knowing that part of me would never sin. An incredible feeling of happiness washed over me, and I knew I was "experiencing roses" again even though there were no roses here. I loved that feeling because my thoughts just stopped, and I was just here. I could never keep this feeling, and if I tried it would just vanish like a genie or a fairy. I never knew when it would come. It just did.

Earlier, I had noticed Bottler Bradley going into the box. Soon we began to realize he was in there for a long time. I was still experiencing my lovely state when I was yanked out of it by Father Daley's voice roaring at the top of his lungs.

"What?!"

Everyone in the church heard it. Over one hundred pairs of eyes were focused on that box. The door slowly opened. Bottler came out sheepishly with his head bowed low. He lifted his head and the shame that was spread across his face quickly changed to confusion when he saw all the attention focused on him. He must have seen the admiration on our faces because a big smile broke across his face as he went to the penance bench.

I got six prayers for my sins, which was considered long for a first confession. Twenty minutes later, Bottler was still kneeling and praying real hard. Every boy in that church was wondering what the fuck he did. We stared at each other, trying to imagine the most terrible deeds. Even Brother Coleman was getting worried, since we had to get back to school. He kept checking to see if Bottler was finished.

Eventually Bottler stood up and smiled again. We had a new hero. Harry said you'd have to commit murder to get that much penance, and the word quickly spread. Nobody messed too much with Bottler since that day.

The school was buzzing with speculation. And as usual it was Harry who revealed the great secret; Bottler was in the IRA. On the walk back to school we had a discussion about what it meant to be in the IRA when Derek called them a load of lousy fuckers.

We all froze in horror at those words. And he looked back at us now in fear, as if we were going to squeal on him and get him kneecapped.

"I didn't mean it! Honest! They aren't lousy fucken' bastards."

We all looked at him doubly shocked.

"How are you expecting to get your first communion tomorrow after saying those filthy words? Those words are mortalers, ya eegit! Now you're not in a state of grace. It's a sin to say lousy fucken' bastards!" yelled Harry.

Then we all looked at Harry. And Harry told us to fuck off because he wasn't really saying it; he was just telling Derek what he said. Derek, nearly in tears, stared at the ground realizing he wasn't in a state of grace and couldn't make his communion. He also knew his ma would kill him when he told her that she wasted all that money on his new suit.

I suggested we ask Brother Coleman if he could go back and make his confession again. They all agreed that this was a good idea, and since it was my idea they decided I should be the one to ask. Proud of my wisdom, I ran on ahead to ask Brother Coleman.

When I caught up with Brother Coleman and explained the situation, he just looked at me as if I was stark raving mad. He asked me to slowly repeat what I had just said. I explained again that Derek Shannon had just committed two mortal sins as we were walking back.

"And where did he commit these sins?"

"Just down there by that lamppost," I pointed out.

"How in the name of God does a boy of seven commit two mortal sins walking down the street and on the day of his first confession?"

Now I was really torn because being in a state of grace I had to tell the truth.

"He called the IRA a bunch of lousy fucken' bastards, twice," I blurted.

Before I had another thought, I got a ferocious slap across the face and was told never to say those words again.

"Get back in line, Brady, and wash out your mouth," he roared, pointing to my place in the line.

I was totally confused. And I was sure I saw him trying not to smile. When I got back to the lads they were just as shocked as I was because they had seen me get slapped.

"What did he say?"

"Can Derek go back to confession?"

There were tears in my eyes from the sting of the blow so I just shrugged and explained that he told me not to use bad language.

"Did you say 'lousy fucken' bastards' in front of a Christian Brother?" exclaimed Harry, shaking his head in disbelief.

"But he asked me what happened, and I'm in a state of grace so I had to tell him the truth," I said, defeated.

"Hey Harry, you just swore," laughed Patsy.

Harry put his fist up to Patsy's face and told him to shut up or he would pop him. This was all very confusing.

Pierce said he didn't believe it was a mortal sin, otherwise Brother Coleman would have brought us back to confession. This was good and we all nodded in agreement, although I knew none of us were sure. And this wasn't good if you were supposed to be in a state of grace.

When I went home that night I felt so good because I was in a state of grace. That meant I had no sins on my Soul, so if

I died that night I would go straight to heaven. My mother asked me what it was like to know that I had no sins on my Soul. I told her I had tried to be good and to love everybody. Trying to be very truthful, I told her that on the way home I saw mean old Bessie Balls in her precious garden, but I couldn't love her, although I tried not to wish that she would die. God! It was hard to love your neighbor. You would have to be Jesus himself to love Bessie Balls, and here I was just a little kid expected to do what Jesus did. Ma just laughed at that and told me not to be stupid. This confused me because she didn't tell me how I was being stupid.

I realized it was very hard to keep free from sin, especially since there are so many of them. When you're in a state of grace, you see how much you are tempted and how hard it is. Going to bed that night I had so many dirty thoughts that I felt filthy. It seemed like I was thinking about everything that I wasn't supposed to think about and I couldn't figure out what was going on. I went to sleep battling with the devil and trying to stay in a state of grace. Tomorrow at my first communion, Jesus himself was going to enter my body. I had to be clean and pure for him and all I could hear in my head were the words "lousy fucken' bastards."

THE DAY HARRY'S DOG ATE JESUS

After I made my Holy Communion, I used to talk to Jesus at night. I asked him why he made me Irish and why he gave me to me da; we didn't get along so well. I mean, I understood why he gave me to me ma and I thanked him for that. Sometimes I'd cry a little bit on me own when I thought of her. I wasn't sad or anything and I never knew what to say to her, but I could feel it. At night I would feel me ma and feel a strange sadness. How can you feel sad and miss someone when you love them and they're not even gone? You're supposed to feel happy, right? It reminded me of something deep inside me, but I could never remember what it was. Jesus and me ma made me cry with happiness – and with sadness. Weird, isn't it?

Anyway, it was thoughts like that that made me wish I could take Jesus out of that old church, where people only went to see him on Sundays, and keep him at home with me. Sometimes I would kneel in front of the big cross and look at him, all that blood pouring out of him. Jesus, how could they do them things to such a nice man? Then I'd remember Brother Coleman telling me Jesus died because of my sins. I'd feel just awful and tell Jesus, all the time, that I was sorry. He got killed because I was a little bastard. Brother Coleman said that every time I lied or committed a sin I was banging the nails into Jesus' hand. Sometimes I couldn't even look at the cross because I felt so bad. If only I could bring him home and help him.

I remember the night Jesus told me how to bring him home. I woke up knowing how to do it. I felt like a saint. I was going to bring Jesus home and make sure no more nails were hammered into him, especially by me. It was simple. Me ma used to buy little tins of germolene, a pink ointment she put on us if we got hurt, cut or scratched. It made you feel better even though it smelled terrible. Anyway, I found a small tin with a little bit of germolene left and brought it to the church.

I was so excited when I saw Father Daley walking to the altar, saying them things priests say when they're putting the Holy Communion in your mouth. You could tell who he liked and didn't like by the way he would say "Dominus Vobiscum." If he didn't like you he would say it through his teeth, but if one of the nice young ones approached he would pause and say it real sincere and holy. I was overcome with emotion as he approached me with the host. I closed my eyes taking Jesus into my mouth. Then I got up off my knees real quick and practically bolted out of the church, like a bat out of hell. Once outside I got Jesus out of my mouth before he melted away and put him in the germolene tin. I was going to clean it out for him, but in a moment of brilliance I saw that the germolene would help him with all the wounds and bleeding. I placed him gently in the tin then put him in my trouser pocket. I had saved Jesus.

Feeling so holy, I walked back into the packed church.

I saw loads of people turning around, wondering where the hell I went. I took my seat beside Harry as he kept staring at me.

"Where did you go to, ya fat git?"

"I was bursting for a piss and had to go." And I added confidently, "Besides it's a mortal sin to piss on the church grounds."

This time Harry couldn't make me feel bad because I knew I was doing God's work and, anyway, I had Jesus in my pocket as proof. I sat back for the rest of the mass feeling like St. Peter himself.

On the walk home Derek started to mess with me a bit, so I turned on him and told him off. "Don't fucken' touch me, right."

Jesus! I said fucken' right in front of Jesus in me pocket. I turned red but the others thought it was from embarrassment for talking like that to Derek. All the way home I guarded Jesus with my life. When I got home I went straight out to the shed in the back garden and opened the tin. He was okay. Now I had him here. Nobody but me and Jesus knew. Jesus had come to Ballyneety Road. Never since "experiencing the roses" had I felt like this. God really existed and he was living in our shed. I hid him under some old papers and went into the house.

"What are you up to?" me ma asked. "And why are ya

lookin' so guilty?"

It was amazing how much me ma knew me, but she would never guess in her wildest dreams what I was up to.

"Nuthin'," I said. I must have looked guilty as hell.

Me ma thought for a minute and let me go. "Sit down there now and eat your dinner."

Just then I thought I heard angels singing out in the shed and I got real scared in case me ma heard them as well.

"What's the matter?"

"Nuthin'."

"He looks like he robbed something," my big sister volunteered.

"Did you rob something?" me ma asked, studying my face.

"No!" But Jesus they were getting close. They could smell blood.

The amazing thing about all this was that I was kind of floating up on the ceiling. It was really weird. How could I be looking at meself? I could still hear the angels singing in the garden, and I could see me sister and ma talking, although I couldn't hear them. I was "smelling the roses" again and this time it was the angels singing that did it.

The interrogation went on for a few minutes until me ma gave up. Knowing she wasn't getting anywhere with me, she told me to go to bed when I finished eating. She was shocked when I said okay and didn't argue with her. After dinner, I went out to the shed to take Jesus to bed with me.

I opened the little tin and there he was. Now we could have great chats. I waited until it was dark and me ma was downstairs before I started to talk. I told him I was sorry for getting him killed, but I was only a kid and didn't know any better. Then something amazing happened. I felt in my heart what he was saying, and I think he was smiling. He was saying, "It's okay, Merv." I didn't hear him with me ears; it was in me chest. I felt his words. I was thrilled; now I knew how God talks to us.

After a few days, when He had soaked up all the germolene, I had another great idea. Every time I got Holy Communion I'd bring him home. Me ma was really suspicious when I told her I wanted to go to bed early every night because I wanted to receive Holy Communion every morning. So for the next two weeks, I was up at seven a.m. to go to the eight o'clock mass for Holy Communion. This also meant I had to be sinless: no lying, no cursing and always doing what me ma and da told me. She must have gone mad wondering what I was up to.

Of course, Harry saw the saintliness in me too, but it wasn't so easy fooling him. He cornered me one day after school and told me to spit it all out. I was dying to tell someone, anyway, so I told him everything from the beginning as he listened in fascination.

"Are you fucken' telling me that you have Jesus Christ himself locked up in a germolene tin in your garden shed?"

he screeched in disbelief. I'll never forget the look on his face.

"Yes," I said bursting with excitement and pride.

"You unbelievable fat bastard! Do you realize what you've done? You're going to burn in hell forever! Locking Jesus up in a germolene tin is a cardinal sin!"

"What the hell is a cardinal sin?"

"It's what you commit if you kill the Holy Father himself."

I was really scared now. Harry was doing it again. I knew I was right, yet he was destroying what I knew was good. Now I wasn't sure anymore. We went to my garden, and I took down the germolene tin. Harry kissed the tin and blessed himself. Then he opened slowly took the lid off as if the bleeding devil was lying there instead of Jesus.

"Oh my God, it's the blessed sacrament."

I never saw Harry like this before. He looked really scared and couldn't move for a few minutes. He was just staring like a mad man. Then I saw his expression changing from fear to deep thought, and I knew we were all right.

"Fatser, you're a genius! Let's get all the fellas on the road to go to communion and get more. Then we can have Jesus in our gang and keep him in my shed."

Harry's shed was bigger and it was where we all hung out, so I agreed.

"Just imagine, Fatser, we'll be the only gang in the world with Jesus as a member!"

He was looking into space when he said that. Even

though I agreed, I was a little disappointed because it meant I had to give Harry my Jesus bodies.

That night Harry's shed was buzzing with excitement. When everyone was quiet Harry told them that a new person was joining our gang on Ballyneety Road. Patsy muttered that he hoped it wasn't a girl or something like that. So when Harry told them it was Jesus, they were all gobsmacked. Before anyone could say anything he took out the germolene tin and showed then the Holy Hosts.

"Fatser, here, found a way to smuggle him out of the church." He went on to tell them the story. He also found a new angle on having Jesus in the gang.

"Just imagine," he said, "we can get whatever we want. We can just ask Him direct, no need to go to the church and pray."

Everyone immediately understood that one. And it was unanimously decided that we'd storm the church for the Holy Hosts – starting tomorrow.

After a week we were well on our way to filling up a big jar full of the bodies. Harry said he should be in a jam jar so we could all see him. All the parents on the road must have been so happy to see their kids transforming into little saints, going to confession and Holy Communion every day.

Now, every morning, when Father Daley would come out to give Holy Communion, he'd stop for a minute and stare at us all lined up to receive the Blessed Sacrament. He'd never guess, not in a million years, what we were really doing. But he could sense that something was up, so he'd glare at us suspiciously while he said "Dominus Vobiscum." Some of us must have looked really uncomfortable and strange as we opened our mouths, remembering Harry's threats that he would beat the crap out of anyone who swallowed Jesus or let Him melt. Then we'd each disappear behind a big statue, where Harry was collecting the Jesus bodies, and reappear with a big, beaming smile. Harry's idea was to wrap up Jesus with the silver wrapping from a packet of his da's Woodbine cigarettes. Then we'd all go back to our seats to pray for a minute and leave. The whole thing must have looked so weird to Father Daley.

After ten days or so, the big glass jar was full of Jesus bodies. The excitement was especially intense one night because we were going to meet to ask Jesus for all the things we wanted. Patsy said he wanted a bike. Derek said he wanted his da to give up the drink. I didn't know what to ask for. I was just happy we were saving Jesus from being alone in the church. Harry and I were sitting in the shed, waiting for the boys to come around at six after tea, when he got the idea to count how many Jesus bodies we had. He got down the jar and poured them all out onto the table.

"Harry! Harry, where the hell are ya?" we heard his father shouting.

We were scared that he would come in because the Holy Sacraments were all over the table.

"Just a minute, da," said Harry running out into the garden.

"Fatser, you come here too I want to talk to you," yelled Harry's da.

We both thought someone squealed on us.

He looked important and intimidating, standing really straight in his army sergeant's uniform. He told us he was helping at the Dublin horse show in Ballsbridge and could get us passes. He also said something about how he and his men would be responsible for putting up the fences that the horses knocked over.

We were so relieved and happy first and then realized what he was saying. We could go there and be with all the toffs and see the horses. Harry asked him if the whole gang could come, and he said no just Harry and one more. We chatted for a while just to be normal and thanked him for the passes. Then Harry's da went in and told Harry to keep the side door locked since he had let Tomahawk, their dog, out in the back garden and didn't want him escaping out of the yard. Harry and I looked at each other and sighed with relief. Our secret was still safe.

As we were going into the shed, Tomahawk was coming out wagging his tale. Jesus! That was one ugly dog. Tomahawk was a big old mongrel with an eye that was looking at something else. He passed us and without any shame started to do a big old shite right in the middle of the garden. We both looked in disgust at the shite, steam still rising out of it.

"You think that's bad?" said Harry putting it into some kind of perspective. "Me da collects that and horse shite and puts it on the cabbage over there. Then makes us eat the fucken' cabbage when it grows."

I was shocked. I was always learning things from Harry. I didn't know cabbage was made from shite. I silently swore never to eat that stuff again. Then we went inside to wait for the boys.

"Jesus! Where is Jesus?" shouted Harry, jumping out of the chair. "He's gone!"

The jar was empty and Jesus was gone. I looked down and saw a bit of Jesus on the floor. And right then, in that shed, I was living the worst moment of my life – worse than the dentist.

"Oh my God!" I exclaimed, terrified, as it began to sink in. "That fucken' dog has eaten Jesus!"

"What?" was all Harry could say, as horror crossed his face.

We both ran outside. There was Tomahawk with his leg cocked, pissing on the cabbage. Neither of us could speak. Sweet Jesus, what was going to happen to us? We were going straight to hell for sure.

The silence was broken with a roar from Harry's father as he bolted out of the house after Tomahawk. "That shaggin' dog all he does is shite and piss in this garden!" he shouted as he laid a strong boot to Tomahawks backside. "How many times have I told you! Don't piss on the cabbage, ya shaggin' bastard."

"Don't kick him, ya can't kick him!" I heard the words coming out of my mouth.

"And why not?"

"Because he has Jesus inside him, and if you kick him you're kicking Jesus."

Harry was looking at me as if I was mad and so was his da.

"What the hell are them priests and Christian brothers teaching you kids nowadays? I'll kick the arse of that dog if it keeps pissing on my cabbage even if the Lord God himself is inside him!" Then he stormed off muttering "fanatic" or something like that.

Harry and I were as white as sheets. We turned to look at Tomahawk who was now giving his balls a good licking. Then that strange feeling of "smelling the roses" came over me, and I wasn't afraid anymore. I could feel how afraid Harry was. I looked at Tomahawk again. He stopped licking his balls, looked straight into my eyes and "smiled." And then, Jesus spoke to me, in that silent way of his. "It's all right, Merv."

The side door opened and the boys came in, smiling. Tonight was the night all their dreams would come true. Then they stopped, dead in their tracks, because Harry and I looked like zombies.

"What's the matter with you two? Have ya seen a ghost

or something?"

Once again my mouth spoke without my permission.

"Tomahawk ate Jesus."

* * *

STUDENT STORY: JAIME
MOMENTS WITH A REMARKABLE MAN

I met Mervyn on Friday, April 12, 2002. I was invited to a conference on art by a friend who was a student of the Fourth way in Mexico City. At the coffee break I waited until Mervyn was alone and approached him.

"How do I know you are awake?" I asked him. It was my only question.

He replied, "Stay close for three days."

I did follow him for three days and he did not forget my question. Quite frequently at the meetings, he repeated my question and used it as teaching material.

The next Monday, I scheduled an appointment, which he required in order to join the newly formed Academy of Mexico City. I arrived at his hotel and I couldn't help but notice a group of women surrounding him like personal guards at the restaurant. Kimiko, a student, told me in her Japanese lilted English, "He will help you to develop your emotional center." Interesting, I thought.

My turn came and I was instructed to go up to his room. I was nervous. What was I going to say? I searched for data, "I am intellectually centered and have a venusian body type*." So

---

* *'Intellectually centered' and 'venusian body type' are terms from an esoteric system, used as tools, to help understand ourselves, others and our relationships.*

103

much for theory. In practice, I knew how to divide my attention (meditative exercise) and so that was what I did. Maybe because of that emotional commitment to divide my attention, Mervyn said when he saw me, "I can see you are present." And inwardly I noted to myself, "So this is it! This is presence."

He was sitting behind a table, barefoot, the leftovers from breakfast – or dinner – on a tray by the floor. The bed was unmade, the curtains were closed and a desk lamp was the only light. I sat in front and tried to remain present, though I did not know what it was. Then, he gave me the look. I was drawn into an intense state unknown to me. I talked and tried to remain present but was unable to hold this intense state. I noted when the presence came back. I do not remember anything of what I said, except that I experienced things that I had only known about intellectually. We talked for about twenty minutes and I felt the urgency for the interview to end; my machine wanted to run, but another part in me could not move. I was in a state of fascination without fear.

I think he saw my state of inner agitation and said, "Remember what you asked me on Friday? Now you know how it feels to be awake. Welcome, I believe you can awaken in this lifetime."

I don't remember what I said – some nonsense about bureaucracy or formalities. I said goodbye and went out of the room. I was ecstatic, as if I discovered the love of my life and kissed her for the first time. I felt exaltation, enthusiasm and energy.

When I got back to the restaurant, Kimiko was the first to notice my change and comment on how I was glowing. I remained there a little while longer...floating. I was literally in love, but with no object. I bid everyone farewell. My body took me to the parking lot, pulled out the car keys, opened the door, and I was there, witnessing how I was opening the door for the first time. I had no choice; I was here. My body operated the car and I could not avoid being there; my thoughts came and went, but the sensation of my hands on the wheel, the clutch pedal or anything physical predominated – that strange sensation of "I am here." I was driven to the bank, crossed the street, went in, filled out a banknote and a check as if using a pen for the first time. Writing was a simple pleasure. I heard the voices, the ambient music and perceived other people. I also felt a kind of shame and vulnerability as if I didn't want to be noticed. My body walked out of the bank, observed the red light and everything on the street at once. Feeling my feet as I walked was an indescribable discovery. I ate, that is, my body ingested food, but I was there, astonished, by my body eating a salad.

That state gradually faded. The experience felt like only twenty minutes, but it lasted for about three hours. I know because due to my skepticism I constantly looked at my watch.

That is how I came to know an illuminated man, a man that is awake. From a former school I had learned that it is difficult to find this kind of connection. Indeed it was Mervyn who gave me his look and not me who looked at him. I had been given the greatest gift. Not theory, but direct experience about something that the mystics of all times have tried to communicate. I had found my Teacher.

At the beginning he called me Jamie (Jay-mee).

"My name is Jaime (Haim-eh)--like James in English," I said.

So I became the quite British James for him and the Academy.

*

One day, while he was looking for a place to live in Mexico City, I invited him for dinner. We knew of his weakness for meat so I treated him to an Argentinian restaurant. We must have eaten a whole cow!

After our first bottle of wine, I saw a very human part about him.

"I honor a man who takes care of his children," he said as he proposed a toast.

My eyes were filled with tears, but I managed to keep my composure. I wanted more wine but I felt embarrassed in front of my teacher, wondering what he would think of me. In hindsight, Mervyn was probably thinking the same thing. Finally, we joyfully ordered our second bottle.

At one point, he accidently dropped his napkin. He bent down to pick it up and as he came back, our eyes met for an instant. I froze and leapt backwards. Mervyn apologized. "Oops, sorry." He was sincere. He had gotten careless and for an instant he left that window opened to eternity or something like that for which I was not ready, not even close to ready, to experience. What I saw were his blue eyes, but what I felt was like an opening to a steel mill furnace. The sensation was of concentrated sun on my skin and tremendous heat energy flowing through my whole being.

We remained silent for a while. I broke the silence by asking something stupid.

"How can I work harder towards my awakening?"

I was not drunk, but that statement came from a drunken man. He reminded me of the question I asked when I met him, and just in that moment, Elton John's song "You'll be blessed" played.

"You see James, that's the signal. That is no coincidence. You are blessed."

Once again my eyes flooded with tears. It was Mervyn who blessed me with is presence and showed me what my soul could be.

On my way home, I felt as if were driving the love of my life to her house after a most incredible evening, an evening where we discovered that "You'll be blessed" was our song. And it was; each time I played it for Mervyn, he would give me a conspiratorial glance, as if to say, "Listen, they are playing our song."

He appointed me Music Director of the Academy in Mexico and also one of his "Intellectual knights."

But what is more precious to me is the day when I looked at him while being present and he said, "You are almost there, James."

* * *

6

BETRAYAL, DEATH & UNDERSTANDING

As the sound of the crash of each wave signals its death
Listen to Souls being released home as the wave
returns to the sea.
The sound of impermanence.
Like death's pulse and heartbeat.
We are terrified of letting go, terrified of living,
Since learning to live is learning to let go.
Let go, let go. Let go, or you will hurt.
Do not grasp at the ungraspable.
Let go, you will not fall.

--Poem shared with Academy, June 1999

THE DENTIST

One morning a white card arrived in the post for my sister and me. Me ma read it to us and said it was great news. We had an appointment with the dentist. Now we could have lovely shiny teeth "just like them film stars."

I never really had any thoughts about shiny white teeth, but me ma seemed happy enough about this so I was happy. I asked her if it would hurt and she told me not to be a big baby that they'd just examine me to make sure I was all right. I had no reason not to be perfectly happy about this, so when I heard I was to get the morning off from school, I was even looking forward to it.

The morning arrived and me ma told us she couldn't come because Mrs. Whealan couldn't come to mind the twins and my baby brother. I was seven and Madeleine was ten, so ma decided Madeleine was big enough to take herself and me.

We got off the bus in Inchicore and walked the mile or so to a huge ex-British army barracks surrounded by great gray stone walls. We entered a big room with wooden benches and three steps leading up to a big green door. I looked around and none of the kids, who were all about our age, seemed worried or afraid. In fact, I recognized some kids from our school. We nodded to each other and smiled.

A big bossy nurse came out and arranged us in alphabetical order. Madeleine and I were fifth in line and were moved onto another bench, closer to the front. She told us the dentist had just come back from his tea and would start seeing us one by one as our names were called.

The first kid went in. Some of us noticed and some of us could care less, swinging our feet and messing around. Two minutes later the door opened and out came the kid, white with fear and holding his face. He was quickly ushered to a vacant seat where he was told to sit quietly and behave himself.

Now we were all paying attention. When the second fella was called in, he was looking a bit unsure. I had no idea what was happening so I tried to take comfort in my ma's words that it would be all right. Then the second fella came out. He had tears in his eyes and was reprimanded by the nurse for being a crybaby. He was plopped down beside the first fella and told to wait. After the fourth fella came out, everyone was paying attention now. Then the first fella's name was called again. The nurse took him by the hand walking him back in and the big green door closed behind them.

What in the name of Jesus were they going to do to him? I looked at my sister, but she ignored me and kept looking at her book. Thirty kids were staring real hard at the door. Four minutes later the door opened and the kid came out. Nothing prepared me for what I'd see next. He was pouring blood out of his mouth. He was holding a big rolled up tissue to his mouth and crying real hard. Oh my sweet Jesus! I wanted to run screaming out of this nightmare, but I knew I wouldn't get past the nurses.

"Brady, Madeleine. Next." And in went my sister.

I was alone in my fear and horror. The kid with the blood was given a white sheet of paper and told to come back in a month. Then he was ushered out the door superfast because the nurse said his whining would upset the other kids.

The door opened again and out came my sister. I'd never seen her looking so white and she gave me pitiful look. Each fella on the waiting bench was called in one by one and came out crying, with blood pouring out of their mouths. So by this point, I was numb with panic when I heard my name.

"Brady, Mervyn."

Time seemed to stand still and everything went real slow. It felt like I was up on the ceiling and could see the whole room. I remember thinking that this is how Jesus must have felt when Pontius Pilate told him he was to going to be crucified. I walked like an angel towards the door, really at peace. I remember thinking my Soul was getting ready to depart because I was going to die. But the moment the door opened, Mervyn the angel left and Mervyn the kid was left staring at a big chair and all these scientific things around it. I recognized that awful hospital smell when I used to go see me da. A huge man with a ruddy face in a white coat had his back to me. He had a big shock of roaring red hair like a big culchie. I'll never forget that impression.

"Sit down there now and let's have a look at the state of ya," he said pointing to the chair.

So this is where I was going to be tortured.

He was fast. One of his big fingers opened my mouth, and he started to say things to the nurse who was busy writing it down. Isn't it strange that when you are about to be tortured you remember hearing words like "extraction," words I had never heard before in my life. Then he told me to open my mouth wide. I nearly fainted with terror when I saw what he was holding in his right hand: the biggest, fattest needle you ever saw in your life. Before I could scream he stuck it right in my face.

God, I'll never forget the feeling of that thing being pushed so far in. Then he turned to the other side of my face and stuck it in again. I could hear myself screaming, but the way he had his fingers in my mouth only I could hear it. I wanted me ma so badly.

"One more should do it," he muttered. And this time the needle went through the roof of my mouth and past my nose. God, I wasn't sure if he would wasn't going to poke out my eye.

"Nurse, take him outside and send in Brady, Madeleine!"

I was so weak from the fright I couldn't stand and almost fainted. The nurse told me to put my head between my legs and I would feel better.

"Come on now, nurse!" I heard him growl, "Take him outside. He can do that there. We're busy, you know!"

I passed my sister who was being led in. We exchanged eye contact like condemned prisoners. I couldn't imagine what they were going to do to her…and how did all the blood get there, anyway? How would Harry handle this? I knew he had never been to the dentist. I remember looking at all the faces of the kids whose names were further down the alphabet. They stared at me with horror and curiosity as if I were a roadside accident.

The nurse sat me down, putting my head between my legs. Then I had a terrible realization – he had cut a lump of my face off and my tongue was gone! My hand involuntarily went to my mouth. It didn't feel like mine. It felt like somebody else's face and tongue. And in a very strange way it felt like "smelling the roses" because bits of me weren't me anymore.

"What do they do to you?" whispered one of the fellas waiting to go, his face frozen with fear.

I was trying to answer him when all I heard was an awful growl. It took me a second to realize that growl was coming from me. I couldn't move my mouth or tongue. What he saw was a babbling idiot, and this only threw him deeper into imagination and despair about his own fate. Spit was running down my mouth, and I realized I was like a madman up in Grange Gorman. I was slobbering all over meself.

The green door opened again and out came my sister with blood all over her piece of cotton wool.

"Brady, Mervyn."

In great moments of danger something happens to you. You know you are going to be done onto and not even God and all his angels or your ma can stop it. The pain goes so deep that you stop resisting. You are totally alone and everything goes silent. I remember forty-four years later seeing the movie "Braveheart." At the end when Mel Gibson is being executed, everything goes quiet when he sees there's nothing more he can do except accept his fate. I knew Mel Gibson must have been to the dentist sometime in his life to be able to portray that moment like he did.

As I walked to the chair, I saw this big beast of a man rummaging through his implements of torture. He chose a vicious pair of pliers and pounced on me. I silently screamed "fuck you!" and "ma, why have you deserted me?" just the way Mel Gibson shouted "freedom!" as he died. Far in the distance, I heard a crunching sound, a loud crack, and I felt his big hand holding my head in place. I knew this is the way I'd feel when I die. I felt warm blood running down my throat and choking me. I was coughing and my head was placed over a little sink with water running out of a little tap.

"Spit in there," I was ordered. Then the pliers came at me again. I screamed silently again as I felt pieces of my face being torn off. I heard the crunching of bone again.

"Spit again. Here rinse your mouth with this."
I was handed a horrible tasting red liquid and a big lump of cotton wool to soak up the blood and then led out by the nurse. As the door opened, I realized that I was experiencing

what it must be like to be in a serious accident. My sister and I were handed two white cards, told to come back in a month, and were pushed out the door.

Outside I leaned against the stone wall and everything hit home in one huge big rush. I started wailing. My sister was crying too, leaning against the wall like me. We just stood there blubbering like babies, for about ten minutes. We couldn't talk and didn't want to. We were in our own private hell, and in the middle of it all I wondered if there really was a God. After a while, we made eye contact, indicating to each other that we should leave.

As we walked down the street an old man walked past and laughed, "Ah, been to the dentist have ya? Sure, that'll make a man of ya."

We stood at the bus stop with our bloody cotton wool to our mouths. People were smiling as if they were glad it was us and not them. They all seemed to know what had happened and thought it was a big joke. Then, I realized that if they knew, then that meant me ma also knew. And with that new thought, I cried all the way home on the bus.

She lied to me and in one stroke severed all my trust in her – and in humanity. I never spoke to her about my experience even when she asked me if I was all right as she put me to bed that night. All I said was "yeah" and rolled over in bed. But I wasn't all right. And then I realized how much I hated words. I wanted to tell her how alone and frightened I was, even before the whole dentist experience.

Now I was ready to talk. I wanted to hug her, to tell her how much I loved her and how much I'd miss her when she dies. I wanted to know who I really was because I knew that there was more to me. I wanted to know who God is and if he really loves us. I wanted to tell her that I would be brave and work with whatever life threw at me, if only I knew for sure God and me ma loved me. I was realizing things that I didn't fully understand; does that make sense? I wanted her to know that everything I had been told was true, that there were reasons for her, for me, and even for the stupid dentist. I was alive and full of possibilities. The wonder of life rose in a crescendo of love for her and for everybody. But all that came out of my mouth was "yeah." As she looked at me, I knew she wanted to tell me about her life, loves, ambitions and failures. But she just said, "goodnight, you have school tomorrow."

I cried myself to sleep and knew I would have to wait until I got to heaven to really talk to me ma. I would have to wait a long time, but I knew she loved me.

THE FIELD MOUSE

One beautiful sunny day, we were playing in the back garden and magic happened.

I was down on my hands and knees by the hedge that surrounded our garden when I saw something so unbelievably great – a little field mouse had crawled over to me.

"Come quick and see what I found!" I called to my sisters.

We were all so happy and touched by this sweet little creature. My sister went inside to get it some bread. We fed it, stroked it and loved it. I picked it up and looked into its little eyes, wondering if mice could think. I made a mental to note to ask Harry about it later. All afternoon we played with it, a real toy, so beautiful and so alive.

When me da came home for his dinner, we ran in to tell him that we had a surprise for him. I was lying on the grass when he came out. I lifted the little blanket we had over the mouse. When he saw it, he ran to the shed and came back with a big spade. To my absolute horror, he pulled back the blanket and bashed the mouse with the spade so hard that it burst in two. I watched the mouse wriggle for a moment. He whacked it again. Then he scooped it up and threw it in the dustbin. That was it. The mouse was dead and gone forever.

"We don't want those bloody things in the garden," he shouted. "They'll be all over the house in days if you let them."

I just sat there, numb, looking at this horrible monster I called my father. How could he have done that to that sweet little innocent mouse?

That shock created another one of those moments when my body and Soul separated. Sometimes, there's an impression that's just too strong and impossible to stomach. That's when I feel that unbearable feeling of being so alone in the world. I turn to an invisible audience for understanding, but nobody is there. The higher part in me observed this savagery without judgement while the other, child, part of me cried because it simply couldn't process it.

Something in me, even at that young age, understood that I was in a cruel world where the rules of the game were very confusing. This slaughter of a tiny, defenseless creature was the most horrific act of barbarism I had witnessed in my young life. I was given a little preview of man's true nature – from me da. I knew I could never justify what he did, and I cried for the mouse. And for myself. Then I was ordered in for dinner.

One thing that I learned that day was that you have to accept things and move on. There were certain things that had to remain unexplained and unanswered. I knew I was too young to understand what had happened. I also knew that one day I would grow into the answer. In great moments of sadness something enters into your blood and changes you. I didn't know it then, but looking back, those were the moments when God, the divine sculptor, shaped my inner world.

I ate my dinner in silence. I noticed my little brother wasn't thinking about the mouse anymore, but was now eating his dinner fearfully, glancing up now and then at my father. I knew he was afraid of him, but I also knew my da wouldn't hit him with a shovel.

THE DEAD HORSE

"My friend to this advice, obey
To the road of truth,
You had best find your way."
-- Author unknown

One day when we were all at school, a big tipper lorry arrived at Jimmy Hogan's house. It was carrying several tons of topsoil for his da's garden. The truck tipped out its load on the side of the street. It would remain there until it was lifted, load by load, into a wheelbarrow and wheeled to the garden. Mr. Hogan signed for the huge mound of fresh soil and admired it, like a child besotted by a new toy. This was going feed all his beloved flowers and shrubs, transforming his front and back gardens. He decided that it would be okay to leave it on the street until he came home that night.

An hour or two later, the Johnson Mooney and O'Brian's breadman came to the street to deliver his daily bread. He was only halfway up the road when his horse just dropped dead, right there on the street.

This stirred up a huge commotion on the road. Loads of the mothers ran out, some of them were even crying. Of course, like any gossip in our neighborhood, the news spread so fast that it reached the gates of our school by the time we were leaving.

We simply couldn't believe it. The horse died right on

our street. How did that happen? We were all in caught up in imagination as we rushed home; of course I arrived much later because I couldn't take the short cut through the bars in the park.

I ran, panting hard. I didn't see the horse, but I saw my friends. They were kneeling in front of Jimmy Hogan's mound of soil, and the crowd of kids kept getting growing as children from other schools gathered.

Harry, with tears in his eyes, looked at me.

"Jesus, Fatser, they've buried him already," he blurted.

I was shocked.

"I didn't know you buried something where it died," I said.

"What do you think they do with all the horses that are killed in the wars? They just bury them, right?"

I felt really stupid and knelt beside him. I began to pray for the horse. Then I was lost for words. I mean what do you say for a horse? He didn't have a Soul (or at least that's what Father Daley had said), so I stole a glance at the others. They all had their heads bowed and were muttering real holy things as if they were at church. I was deep in my thoughts when I heard Mary Hogan's voice shouting at us.

"What the fucken' hell are you lot doing to me da's topsoil?"

Derek looked up piously and in a hushed voice reminded her not to be so common because we were praying at the grave of the dead horse.

* * *

STUDENT STORY: HOLLY
EMAIL FROM MERVYN, OCTOBER 2005

Dearest Holly,

It must have been a big shock for you.

Remember you have only one father, and in his departing, he can impart a great gift onto you.

Pushing deeper the realisation that this life is but a short time, we don't know the time when we arrive or depart.

I have no advice to you, simply because there is nothing for you to do.

There is no point in me reminding you to be present as this is real suffering and the outcome will be that you will now verify that there is something in you which will rise up in the face of suffering.

Self-remembering will be done onto you. You have no choice.
We need these external shocks to inflame our inner world.

I know you are ok and growing.

Try to maximise your father's parting gift and allow it to penetrate you, just the way you have allowed love to.

Francis and Rylie live in San Diego in an area called La Jolla. I wrote to them and they are there to help you in any way they can.

They want to help and also to meet you if you have some time... Please call them if you can.

I am completely with you and will make every effort I can to be close. Think of me and be strong...

I love you so much.
Mervyn

* * *

7

WISDOM AND KNOWLEDGE

The learned and studious of thought do not have a monopoly on wisdom. Their often single-minded pursuit of intellectual knowledge, in many ways disqualifies them to truly think.

We get many valuable observations from people who are not very profound, yet they often say things without effort... inspired things, which we have often been hunting for in vain.

The action of the Soul is better felt, and left unspoken. We always know better than we DO. Man does not yet possess himself, yet he knows that he is much more than he is.

The Soul of man is present in all periods of his life, just as much in the child as in the adult. In dealing with children, who we are and what authority we have means very little. Our position in society is lost on them, but the more we show them our Souls, the more they notice. If we impose our will on a child, it will only set their will against ours... and we lose when we impose our superior strength on them. We should forget all the do's and don'ts of our perceived parental duties and act from the soul instead... my daughter's eyes look into my Soul, and she reveres and loves me.

The Soul is the perceiver and the revealer of truth. It knows truth when it senses it...let the foolish say whatever they will. We are wiser than we know. The Soul passes into and becomes that creature that it enlightens... directly in proportion to the creature's ability to receive the Soul.

Often when the Soul speaks, man calls it revelation. This is a downloading of the Divine mind into our mind. A thrill passes through all men at the reception of new truth. When higher centers manifest, the power to see and understand becomes connected to the will to do and the doing comes from a joyful obedience of the creature.

When a man awakens, the man speaks with a changed tone. His speech becomes plain and true. He treats all men as God would, accepting, without any admiration or judgement.

The simplest person, who genuinely seeks God, becomes God.

--Excerpt from "Thoughts of the Soul"
Journal, September 2000

TRINITY COLLEGE

At the center of Dublin, there's a great big building surrounded by tall green railings. This is Trinity College Dublin. I used to wonder why you had to say "Dublin;" where else was it? Often when I was in town, I'd imagine what mysterious things went on in there. What awesome secrets of learning were inside?

Once Harry told me that this was the place where Frankenstein went to school. "They chop up people's bodies in there and experiment on them, Fatser." We were always real careful when we walked by. Once we saw a fella in a white coat through one of the windows, so we knew Harry was right.

The great wooden doors at the entrance represented everything posh and English. The students and experimenters didn't talk like Harry and me. Sometimes I'd go up to one of them to ask the time, just to listen to the way they'd talk. It was amazing how they could speak without moving their face, only their mouths. And you always felt like a real fucken' eejit because they could make even telling you the time sound so important. Sometimes I'd walk away thinking, Jesus! It's three o'clock.

My mother told me the green railings were to keep the likes of us out and protect the students from Dublin gurriers. She'd say that you had to be a gentleman or the son of a gentleman to go there. She'd say this with pride, as if knowing this gave her some insight into the secrets of Trinity College.

One day, I was carrying suitcases for an American couple from the bus stop to Kingsbridge Station when they told me they had visited the College.

"How did you get in?" I asked, amazed.

They looked at me as if I were moron and replied that they just walked through the front door.

"It's open to the public. Haven't you ever been there?"

I felt cheated. All these years of passing by that big gate, wondering what happened in there, and now Americans, once again, were telling me about my own town. I suppose people from Ballyfermot never really thought much about going in there. And even if they did, they probably didn't have the guts to walk past the uniformed guard at the gate. I always thought he was there to keep the likes of us out. Any big building in town with a uniformed guard was to keep us out. We all knew that.

The next day, I entered the gate, walking past the guard and trying to look like I did this all the time. He actually said, "Good morning, sir," as I passed.

Ah, the power of inside information.

I entered into the College courtyard, a big square that I never knew existed. People were walking around with books, talking real important, and none of them looked like they were from Ballyfermot. There were lots of lovely girls sitting around talking. None of them were shouting or laughing real loud. You knew they weren't like the girls on our street because none of them had high heels or combed back hair. Many of the fellas had glasses and sport jackets. I always wanted one of them, especially the ones with the leather bits at the elbows.

I fancied myself as a posh student. Then I wondered why so many of them had glasses. Maybe Madge Cox would fancy me if I had a Harris tweed jacket and glasses. Harry once told us that men with glasses had the biggest mickeys and that's why women love them. I made a mental note to borrow my father's glasses. Then I spent the next minute feeling sick, wondering if that was the reason me ma married him.

The next memory I have is standing in the middle of the great library. Jesus! I'd never seen anything like this in my life. I could smell the books. It was a musty smell that made you think of school, only this time I couldn't believe what I saw – rows and rows of books, some so big you couldn't carry them around. I hungered so much to study and learn. I felt a wave of sadness, and then a wave of great injustice and anger. All this was denied me because my parents were poor and Irish. I looked around at the shelves of books, stretching from floor to ceiling. I was surrounded by knowledge, thousands of volumes on hundreds of subjects, books so large it'd take me ages to read one. Then all I felt was awe in my new realization.

My brief life on this planet was simply too short, my

head too small, to hold all this knowledge. How do you possibly learn it all? I began to suspect my own nothingness and mortality. Here I was, surrounded by the emblems of human achievement, collective knowledge that was much too big for one poor Irish kid. Jesus! In the face of all this, how do you become wise?

Even if, at that very moment, I began to diligently read all the books in the rest of the time I had in my life, I'd maybe make inroads into only nine or ten meters of ceiling to floor worth of books. I'd only succeed in becoming a deranged intellectual only able to parrot stuff on electromagnetism, or whatever subject happened to be where I was standing. Wanting to be learned and wise was like trying to eat and digest a wall, brick by brick, book by book. I'd become so busy trying to digest all this knowledge that I'd end up understanding nothing.

I saw a load of people looking at something so I went over where they were looking at an old book in a glass case. They were collectively cooing over it. Yes, you guessed it; they were all American tourists. When they moved on, I stared at this old book for a long time. The colors were brilliant and you could see that an awful lot of trouble was taken to write each letter. It was really old, written by monks thousands of years ago, called the "Book of Kells." They must have had a lot of time on their hands in those days. Now, the wise fellas are priests, not monks, and priests wouldn't spend that kind of time with one book.

These fellas didn't spend their lives reading thousands of books. No, these monks spent their lives writing one. Clearly these monks didn't have the same problems I had. They lived in nice monasteries and didn't have to be home for their tea, or have girl problems. All they had to do all day was hang out, pray to God to make them even holier than they already were, and write a page every six months or so. They had it easy.

I was starting to understand one of the great secrets: if a man wished to become wise, getting knowledge was only part of the process. I saw that if his ability to understand got out of pace with what he was learning, he'd end up parroting "pretty polly," teaching kids pretty much nothing, and understanding nothing. Now I began to despair. It was obvious that even if my parents were rich and English, I couldn't eat the library.

I left the library, my head spinning with strange new thoughts, and found myself back in the courtyard. I saw a crusty old man with a balding head, thick glasses, stooped at the shoulders and looking like he needed a good feeding. He was carrying an armful of heavy books, scurrying out of the library like he had stolen them. He was grinning and muttering to himself like he had gone mad from reading too much.

Something inside me singled him out as the "one who had begun." He was on the "way." He had found the path to wisdom. He was holding onto the books the way I would desire puddings when I was in hospital. Jesus, he was thrilled with himself. He had started the madman's way: this week, six books and next week, six more. I thought I could see the strain on his face from all that reading. Then I wondered if he ever screwed a girl, and in that moment he became my hero. What must he have sacrificed to keep learning? He probably made this decision at some point early in his life and now was devoted to "eating the library." He probably earned his daily bread by teaching other young hopefuls who had come to dine on books as well.

Speaking of bread, he now sat down on the lawn and spread his two meals in front of him, the sandwiches and the books. He was completely unaware of my fascination with him, so I slid closer to observe my new hero. I also took a good long look at his crotch to see any signs of a big mickey, since his glasses were really thick. I didn't notice any signs of a big mickey, though I did see that he had a cheese sandwich in one hand and was turning the pages of a big book with the other.

The book was "The Sermons of Meister Eckhart." Many years later I learned Eckhart was a German mystic. I was impressed with this new bit of information and continued reading the other titles. Then I stopped in horror with another realization. Not only was he reading this huge book on Meister Eckhart, but there were many other books about the first book, just as big: books about the first one, another book disputing the second, the third explaining the virtues of the fourth, and so on. Jesus! Books about books!

Right then, I knew that I'd try to read Meister Eckhart myself. I wouldn't start reading what every other bugger had to say about him. This way I could decrease the amount of books I would have to read by fivefold. I'd go back to the source so I only had to read the real thing. His way, you'd go around and around in circles reading what every other eejit thought. I trusted that the wise men of the past would want to speak directly to me through time and space. I'd dig them up and not tell anyone. I didn't have to be rich or English to understand them. These wise fellas would be my teachers, and I knew that they wouldn't mind that I hadn't been to secondary school. They belonged to ordinary people, too. I'd get them to teach me and nobody could stop me.

There were no professors around when Socrates was figuring out his stuff. The fellas good old Socrates talked to didn't need a professor to explain his words. These bastards with the glasses had taken over the wise men the way the British had taken over Ireland, the way the priests had taken over God.

I was getting really pissed off with the old man, now. I wanted share these realizations with Harry and the guys on the street. I looked at my ex-hero with disdain, realizing he wasn't aware of anything besides his books. He didn't feel the sunshine. He didn't know I'd been watching his every move, and he didn't have a clue that he'd just been sussed.

As I got up, a deep and familiar sensation moved

through me. I felt really happy. I walked away looking back at the old man sitting on the grass; now he looked like a dung beetle, consuming his books and sandwiches with the same frantic energy. I skipped a little, feeling that it was great to be alive and walking on the soft grass – a little brat from Ballyfermot, in Trinity College, walking around as if I owned the place. Filled with daring, I made a promise to myself that I was going to find all the masters, read everything they wrote and become wise. Then in the middle of my vow, I noticed this pretty little thing sitting on the grass. Jesus! You could see her knickers!

At that moment, I must have gotten lost somewhere in my head because, for the life of me, I can't remember what happened next. It'd be years later that I'd recall the lessons learned that day and remember that Socrates and Meister Eckhart were waiting for me patiently on a bookshelf.

THE MUSEUM

I was out on my own one day, wandering the streets of Dublin. I had left St. Stephens Green and decided to go down a street I hadn't been down before. I was on Kildare Street when I came across this impressive building. It said "entrance free" on the railings outside and I saw lots of American-kinds of people going in. I say "American-kinds of people" because they had raincoats and umbrellas, and you could hear them talking from real far away. They also all had that look on their faces as if they'd just arrived from the planet Mars and knew nothing about Earth. They'd look at the buildings as if they'd never seen one before, touching the railings as if they'd just discovered metal. They kept saying "cute." One couple, wearing matching cream-colored raincoats, stopped to stare at me. I felt like a monkey at the zoo.

"Gee, honey, just look at that little Irish boy, isn't he cute?"

The really interesting thing was that the "American-kind of people" always knew what was going on. So I figured if they were going in there, there must be stuff worth looking at. So I went in. The policeman guarding the door looked at me, and I thought he was going to tell me to fuck off. I automatically assumed he was there to stop little shits like me from going in, so I couldn't believe it when he opened the door for me. I remember thinking that he must have thought I was an American.

I was gobsmacked when I went through the big doors. I couldn't believe my eyes. There was a huge room filled with the most beautiful costumes in glass displays. Everywhere I looked, there was the most amazing stuff filled with things I had never seen before. The past was staring me in the face – uniforms of the Irish Republican Army, all those amazing clothes that army officers from the past used to wear, all those beautiful jackets. To think that they went to so much trouble to look nice when they were killed. It made me almost forgot that that was how they dressed to kill people. Over on the other side were things like flints and spears, things that people used to use as weapons five thousand years ago. There were even everyday things they used like pots and jars.

Something was very familiar with all of this—it was like hearing a piece of music for the first time that you can hum along with and wondering how you already know it. It made me think about death because the fella that made this bowl or that spear was long dead. Something deep inside me knew that only his body was dead. I wondered where the rest of him was now. In that moment, I wouldn't have been surprised if an angel popped out of thin air and told me the poor fella's spirit was still hovering around his bowl. And in the middle of the old pottery and kitchen utensils, I experienced that lovely familiar feeling of floating again.

In this lovely state, I wasn't prepared for what I would see next. As I peered through a big glass display, I saw, with revulsion and fascination, a skeleton of one of the original Irish people. He was lying on his side. He seemed so alone here, away from his family with all these strange living people looking at him. I wondered how he died and I felt so sad that, despite myself, tears ran down my cheeks. Here I was, a nine-year-old kid, confronted with death and eternity. I couldn't take my eyes off him. One minute I was walking around without a care in the world, and the next I was staring at this man in a box, dead for hundreds and hundreds of years. I could see that this other, eternal part of me was really watching everything at that moment. I remember wishing that I could be more a part of this moment, but all my body could do was just stare, while this other part of me observed.

How was it possible that I never knew about this place? How come the boys and me never even heard of this place? And it was free. I never even heard the word "museum" before. How did all these Americans know it was here? Was there a conspiracy to keep poor Dublin kids from knowing what was under our noses? I was getting really pissed off.

Looking at that skeleton was, for me, like looking into the abyss. I tried to go on to other things in the museum, but I just couldn't take them in. In the poor skeleton I saw everything about death. To me, he represented the Irish nation and human civilization. I simply couldn't fathom that I could die, but I knew my body would die and become like his one day. The fear and panic was unbearable, so I finally forced myself to look at other things.

139

On my way out, I passed solid gold plates and real posh knives and forks; there was gold and silver everywhere. I knew what gold and silver was supposed to look like, but this place was overflowing with the real stuff. Some of it belonged to rich Irish, but most of it belonged to English lords and ladies.

It made me sad, thinking about our little house with our mismatched crockery, left to us from various aunts. These people must have been so filthy rich, and here I thought Harry's parents were rich. How does this happen? How do you become that rich? There was obviously a whole world that I knew nothing about, or worse, one that nobody bothered to tell me about. Amazing what a man could do. I also felt a little ashamed for being so ignorant and judging the Americans. I made a mental note to watch where they go in the future since they seemed to know all the best places. The world and human history was so enormous, and for the first time I sensed the insignificance of my life in Ballyfermot.

I left the museum, thrilled. I'd discovered a great secret, an Aladdin's cave, and I couldn't wait to tell the lads. I felt a little like Christopher Columbus discovering the Americas. There was just so much you had to know to be wise. But at least I was on my way.

I ran all the way to Harry's house and told him to get all the kids together for a meeting. When we convened in Derrick Shannon's shed, I explained everything I'd discovered on my journey into the big city. None of them knew what a museum was, so I enlightened them. They listened amazed as they heard all about treasures beyond their wildest dreams, but the winning story was the skeleton. At first they didn't believe me and kept asking if you could really see it. But when they were finally convinced, we looked at each other solemnly acknowledging the importance of this find. Unanimously it was decided that there wasn't any time to waste. Tomorrow we'd go off to the museum, where we'd embark on our voyage into the unknown.

RAID THE COFFERS OF THE LEARNED

I didn't know it then, nor did I know what the word was, but I was becoming a "philosopher." Later, I understood that, translated from its Greek origins, it meant "a lover of wisdom."

Maybe all children are philosophers, but their mothers give them too many stupid answers. Perhaps it was our parents, the nuns and priests, and all the other sneaky, unexposed traitors of true knowledge who stifled our budding curiosity – namely, the professors. The professors, the keepers of knowledge, whittle away the treasures of human understanding and steal them away to their ivory towers. There, they complicate what little they understand, claiming it with intellectual garble and pass it along to their peers. They squabble and praise each other in their exclusive circle while they hold the legacy of understanding, the birthright of every member of the human race, under lock and key. More than the well-meaning priest or the tired mother, the professors have held back the Soul of humanity. They have managed to perfect an intellectual arrogance that pours water on the fire of the true seekers knowledge. They are like knowledge lenders – if you pay their institutions large amounts of money, they will grant you an indulgence, like the medieval popes.

To the great mass of people out there, I urge you, in the strongest possible way, to become real men and women.

With the questions of your Soul, take charge of it. Seek out good, robust company, the kind you can respect and truly learn from. Don't seek answers from these scoundrels who have stolen our legacy of beauty and knowledge. You will pay tremendous amounts of money and spend half your life learning huge amounts of useless knowledge, while your inner world slowly starves.

Don't get me wrong, there should be places of learning, but the professors should be treated for what they really are, passers of knowledge, and must rescind their ambitions to teach the whole man. When universities first came into being, they purported to teach the whole man, including his Soul. In the late twentieth century, the university is slightly above a polytechnical school. Like her sister, the Church, Academia has crystallized and is no longer able to change and adapt. Ironically, it's in the sciences that she has not crystallized, as most scientists don't yet have the audacity to claim the last word on their areas of expertise.

Philosophy, once the science of kings, men and gods, has now been relegated to the lowliest discipline. There are too many arrogant professors who claim to be experts on great men of truth like Plato, Aristotle, and Seneca. They are fleas writing about giants, so they squabble about the details and words while missing the truth. Mired in their ignorance, yet insisting that they hold the secrets of the universe, they are tiny men trying to explain only what a fully developed Soul can understand.

THE STORY OF ST. AUGUSTINE

I am reminded here of the great story of St. Augustine, who meditated for years in his splendid monastery. One day as he walked along the beach, he saw a young boy digging a hole.

"What are you doing, boy? Why are you so fervently digging that hole?" the great saint asked him, condescendingly.

"I'm digging a hole that all the sea can flow into," replied the young boy.

"Don't be silly, boy. Anyone can see that the ocean can't possibly fit in that hole," laughed the saint.

At this point, the boy transformed into an enormous, beautiful angel.

"There's more chance of the ocean filling that hole than the secrets of God and His Holy Trinity fitting into your head!" rebuked the angel.

As a young boy, it meant so much to me when I discovered this story in a painting. It told me that the secrets of the universe will always remain aloof to man, that no matter how hard he struggles, truths belong to the Soul. Unless a man or woman first connects with their own Soul, knowledge, no matter how powerful, can't change a single thing. All the wisdom, left to us from the great philosophers of the past, are only words to the body. But to the inner world, it is the fuel to life and a map to the Soul.

There is a Tibetan saying, If you become too intelligent, you will miss the point. Professors have faithfully passed along wisdom in sealed envelopes from generation to generation. In those rare moments when we dare open the envelope, we are pecked to death for our audacity.

Remember, Jesus said, "Unless you become like little children, you will not enter the kingdom of God." I remember the day when I understood those words. I thanked him so much for my wonderful childhood. I vowed to guard my children's childhood for them and not to speed them into the world of adults and the body. I promised myself that I would talk to them about fairies, angels and leprechauns, all the strange and wonderful creatures who share this splendid world in another place, very close to us. Within the open-hearted wonder of a child lies the key to heaven.

* * *

STUDENT STORY: REBECCA

There is a Buddhist phrase, "When the student is ready, the teacher will appear."

I met Mervyn during the grief-shrouded months that had followed the tragic passing of my sister, Jeannie, who at only eighteen, had been killed instantly when an impaired driver hit her side-on. He told me the enduring pain of the shock was the friction that was awakening my Soul. He understood I was ripped wide-open, and that my grief had torn through all the layers of my soul's epidermis, leaving me bare and vulnerable.

He taught me that "self-remembering is self-preservation" and that my "suffering was a gift not to be wasted." Through his teaching, he facilitated the planting of my grief seeds in the soil of my Soul.

I became Mervyn's student and my real Work began. With grief mirroring Love, Mervyn helped me transform the the fruits of suffering into food for my inner world. With his tutelage, I began to observe myself and learn what keeps me asleep and trapped by habitual recurrence.

In Mervyn's Conscious School, he shared his interpretations of Renaissance art, explaining the symbolism and how each painting related to the journey of the Soul. He taught me that beautiful impressions are food for the Soul, and showed me how to remain present.

Above all else, Mervyn's teaching was Love. Love casts out all fear. Love awakens. Love regenerates. Love transcends.

I remember Mervyn saying, "Self-remembering is consciousness loving you into existence."

As I meditate, surrounded in beauty and stillness, I honor my Teacher through my own self-remembering. And in this sacred space, my Soul understands his words once again.

Love is the way.

* * *

8

LEARNING TO STAND IN THE WORLD
(Punishment stories: ages 5 to 11)

What would you think if I told you that –

I fought in a battle and you were there with me?
You were my army of angels… but we lost.

And being defeated,
we were assigned an exemplary punishment.
From being Light,
to the prison of condensed matter.
Trapped in it… crystalised.
And in this dense state… mineralised.
We were confined to a faraway place in the universe,
In a forgotten galaxy, far from the center of the universe,
in a place called Earth.

Very slowly we emerged towards the surface.
Thousands of years later our souls, in human bodies,
began to evolve.

Finally the moment has arrived,
by Divine mandate, at this moment in time -
The sentence is over.

And people like me, wise men, we have come to remind you:

The prison no longer exists!
We can escape.
There is no reason to stay here any longer.
But in order break free, we have to awake from this dream.

Our souls can return to God.
We have been forgiven.
And they are waiting for us to return back to the Light.
Free at last!

Part of the beginning of the way back is to help each other,
To aid in the process of awakening.
We belong to each other, the same species.
That is why I came back.

Remembering your Soul, your job is being completed!
There is no more pressing business here on Earth.

Nothing is more important than this!

--Hanging out with students in Polanco, Mexico, 2002

SISTER MARY *(Age 5)*

As with all children in Ballyfermot, I was sent to the nuns at the Dominican Convent. As far as I can remember, we weren't punished very much there, probably because we were only five-years-old. But I do remember Sister Mary Aloisius did carry a strap under her lovely cream and black habit.

One day a boy wouldn't come in from the playground, and Mrs. Murray, one of the teachers, asked Sister Mary to bring him in. Sister Mary pulled him in to the classroom and, with the speed and precision of a skilled executioner, she held his hand in one of hers and produced a big, thick, leather strap about half an inch thick. She raised it up above her head and brought it down, full force, on his hand.

The pain and shock of the blow knocked all the fight out of him. I'll never forget the look on his face: nothing could have prepared him for that kind of searing pain. It was probably the first time in his life he was punished like that. A second slap was brought down on his little hand. The poor kid went very still, and then tears poured down his cheeks.

Strange for a little boy to be a screaming, kicking animal one minute and the next, to be feeling sore and sorry for himself. The boy was ordered to his desk. He sheepishly sat down, nursing his hand and sobbing quietly.

The effect on the rest of us was unbelievable. We'd never seen anyone punished in cold blood like that; I knew that the next time the bell rang, I'd be in line and go straight into class. Every child there learned his lesson, and no one challenged Sister Mary Aloisius after that.

We had witnessed a public execution and the message was clear. But I still didn't know all the rules of the game, and it would be only a matter of time before it was my turn to get the strap. Sister Mary liked me, often telling me that she wished there were more boys like me in the school, but I wasn't fooled. I knew how bad I was – she just hadn't found out yet.

One day we were talking about loving God first and then your parents. Sister Mary asked me in front of the whole class who I loved after God. I answered, "You, Sister." I'll never forget the look on her face. She turned a lovely shade of pink and smiled like an angel.

Ah, the power of vanity. I didn't even know the word yet, but my Soul observed the whole thing and noted it well. I fell in love with her in that moment. And I saw that love was raw honesty and unleashed when declared.

Sister Mary was always clean and crisp, her face was beautiful like a saint's and she smelled of clean starch. She knew everything, and I was convinced she was a goddess. I was only five, but I was in love with a beautiful woman whom I feared and loved at the same time. I wanted to be with her all the time, so often after school I'd walk over to the convent with her. I didn't know what I wanted from her;

life hadn't taught me the right words, so I just looked at her silently, adoringly, like a love struck puppy.

When we arrived at the big doors, she'd tell me to go home because only nuns were allowed through the door. That place fascinated me. It had immaculately polished wooden floors and was really clean. Just inside the door was a big statue of Jesus with big white flowers. I would have loved to go in and be holy. As I reluctantly walked towards the gate, I longed to belong to the convent and to be close to Sister Mary. Whenever I thought of her, I was filled with silent, wordless longing, strangely sweet and sad. It reminded me of something I had somehow lost but couldn't remember how. Then I'd see my ma waiting for me and forget, happy to see her.

.

WHIPPED DOG SYNDROME *(Age 7)*

When we were seven, we heard horror stories about what was waiting for us when the girls and boys were split up. The boys went across the road to the De La Salle Christian Brothers. We heard they punched you if you made a mistake and that if you cried, you got the cane. I wondered what a cane was.

I quickly learned all about canes, and after the first time I saw one in action, learned to fear them. It was a long bamboo stick about three and a half feet long and half an inch in diameter, and you could hear it swish as it cut through the air.

"Six of the best" were the dreaded words. If that was your punishment, you had to go to the front of the classroom and take it like a man. You decided which hand was sacrificed first. You had to hold out your arm, fully extended at shoulder height, and open your hand, palm up.

A Brother would take aim, raise the cane above his own shoulder and whack you, full force, across your palm. This was excruciatingly painful. The cane was raised again. The second one penetrated your mind, and no matter how brave you felt, you were in big trouble at this point. If you flinched and tried to pull your hand away, you got an extra whack. After three blows, you had to sacrifice your other hand to the same process.

If the Brother wanted to hurt you even more, he'd hold

you by the wrist to make sure your hand fully absorbed the stroke. He'd strike the cane across your finger tips or the joints on your fingers instead of the palms. I frequently saw boys with black and blue fingers.

When you were sent back to your desk, you were expected to pick up your pen to write or draw. The resilience of children still surprises me. When a boy was being thrashed, all you could think was "Thank God it's not me."

To this day, I can't come to terms with how adults could do that to children.

Imagine a fully-grown man thrashing the little hand of a child with all his strength, inflicting severe welts that would almost cripple the poor child for days. What's most disturbing was that this was sanctioned by the government, and, even worse, the Holy Catholic Church. As children, there was nobody to turn to, so we had to just accept it.

As the years passed, it only got worse. In our third year, we had a teacher who was not a Brother. We were considered lucky that we were to have such a progressive teacher.

Sure, he was progressive; he had found a new way to inflict pain. His new approach was a twelve-inch wooden ruler, held sideways. When your hand was extended, he would slam the ruler down across your fingers, not the palm. It made a bonking sound as it hit the bones of your fingers; the boys used to howl with pain. They'd have thin black and blue lines across their fingers for days.

The worst thing that could happen was to have to get

"six of the best" again, the next day, before your hands had time to heal. This was sheer torture, and boys begged not to get hit again on their injured hands. This was usually interpreted as insubordination, so the punishment was given with greater gusto.

I remember one boy screaming in pain, and the teacher slapped him across the face.

Sometimes I would quietly cry and swear at God. Everything was geared to serve God in school, and I couldn't understand how He could let things like this happen.

The day came when it was my turn to taste this new punishment. After the first bone crunching blow, I involuntarily curled my hand to soften the blow, so when the ruler came down, it caught the nail on my middle finger, almost tearing it off. The brother caught my hand and made me straighten it out, then proceeded with the punishment. Then he switched to my other hand and continued the torture.

There is pain that stays on the surface, like on the palm of your hand. Then there is the kind of pain that penetrates deep inside your being. If that kind of pain overcomes you, you hurt deep down in a defenseless and vulnerable place. For me, that point came after the second blow. I howled in agony like a wounded beast, all semblance of control abandoned. I hated this sadistic spectacle: boys reduced to tears and broken in spirit.

Now, as a man, I sometimes encounter a certain type of

Irish man with a certain countenance I call the "whipped dog syndrome." He speaks quietly, won't argue and has a slight stoop to his shoulders.

When my mother saw my black and blue hand that evening, I knew that a terrible storm had been unleashed. I'd never seen her so angry and didn't know what to expect when she went to the school the next day. There was an excited buzz through the class when my mother barged in and showed the brother my hand. I was told to sit down. Then they went out into the corridor. I could hear my mother shouting at him and his faint, muffled protests.

He returned to the class ten minutes later and carried on as normal. After class he told me to stay back because he wanted to talk to me. He apologized for the damage to my nail but also told me that it was my own fault for not opening my hand properly.

He never hit me again.

I was grateful for my mum, but there were many boys who didn't have my kind of mother or father. Perhaps they were at work. I really can't remember another mother complaining about her son's punishment.

We were taught almost everything in Irish, a language none of us could speak. So it was easy to make a mistake, and I couldn't ask my parents to help me because they didn't speak Gaelic either.

This was the only thing that used to catch Harry. He

was great at everything, but he just couldn't get the hang of the Irish language. The teacher would yell at him, asking him if he was stupid, and demand an answer in Irish. Harry invariably made mistakes and was ordered up front for a caning. I remember wishing that I could speak for him.

At the end of the year, we all felt relief and sadness. Despite everything, that teacher did seem to really care for us. Perhaps nobody was to blame; we just had to get on with it. It just was the way it was.

BROTHER NELSON *(Age unknown)*

Brother Nelson was a clean cut man who always smelled of aftershave, had immaculately tidy hair and shoes so shiny you could see your reflection in them. He would make you stand to read from a book, and then he would put his hand up your shorts and play with your privates.

We couldn't for the life of us figure out why he would do that. I mean for Christ's sake why would you want to put your hands up a fella's shorts? We used to laugh about that.

I remember one day Brother Nelson was discussing Jesus and the Apostles, about how much they loved each other and how they would do anything for each other. He asked us if could we love like an apostle, and like eegits we all nodded in unison and said yes.

He stared at you when he asked these questions, and I had a bad feeling. I knew he wasn't asking what he was asking. I was always wary in case I gave the right answer to his true, unasked question. In hindsight, I see that a child is not totally unaware of these subtle but threatening situations. We knew there was something wrong, but uncertain what it was, we laughed at him. Yet we remained wary. Fortunately, I never heard about him crossing beyond these already inappropriate boundaries.

FINNBAR FURY *(Age 10 or 11)*

Our next class was with Brother Coleman. If he's still alive, he'd better have been doing a lot of praying, because there are a lot of boys out there whom he wouldn't be safe from, even in heaven. He was a tall, dark-eyed man who wore spectacles and looked like a medieval inquisitor. He was infamous, and we knew we were in for it way before setting foot in his class. He was known for catching you by the sideburns and almost lifting you off your feet. He'd come around the desks to check your work, and if he wasn't impressed, you got your sideburns pulled. The temple is a very tender part of the head, and he'd cause even greater pain by twisting it until you yelped.

We were around ten or eleven-years-old at this time and were beginning to develop our various characters. One day he threatened a boy with "twelve of the best" and to my horror a boy stood up to him and said that according to the law, you can't give more than six. Incensed, Brother Coleman ordered the boy up to the front of the class. I'll never forget that day or that boy. His name was Finnbar Fury, the gypsy. I thought the big kid was an idiot, for not knowing how to play the game.

Brother Coleman said he was going to give him "twelve of the best" for his cheek, and to show him it wasn't against the law. Finnbar put out his hand and didn't even flinch as the third stroke came down. He had a grim, hard look of determination. I remember being amazed at his bravery and strength of character. The fifth and six were too much for him, and tears ran down his cheeks. But he didn't cry out.

But Brother Coleman was determined to break him, so he grabbed Finnbar's other hand by the wrist and slashed away six times at his hand. Still, Finnbar refused to cry out. When the punishment was over he put his hands under his arms and walked back defiantly to his seat.

We wanted to stand and cheer for him. I'd never seen anything like it. That day I learned about gross injustice and the power of the human spirit. The courage of one boy had defeated an entire establishment. In Finnbar I had a new hero. This was a turning point in my life, and I have him to thank for it.

On the playground, all the boys flocked around Finnbar, asking to see his hands. We knew he was a bit of a musician and wondered if he would play again. He was okay, although his hands were raw and bloody. Brother Coleman's spell seemed to break after that; I feel Finnbar brought him to his senses.

Many years later when I was living in Spain, I heard some great Irish music playing in a bar, so I asked the owner who the group was. "The Fury's" he said showing me the album cover. Imagine my surprise when there, in the picture, was Finnbar Fury, my old classmate and hero.

* * *

STUDENT STORY: MICHAEL
LETTER FROM MERVYN, SUMMER 1995

Dearest Michael,

It is Monday Sept. 7, 13:30 hours.

I am sitting in "The Crypt" a 1700's coffee shop under a church in Trafalgar Square.

I read your letter with great interest and felt your rare pain of seeing oneself. People who never work beyond their own name are the ones who usually give such stinging advice and criticisms.

Last night I hardly slept as I received a message from one student informing me that she was angry with another student for not confiding in her about a certain situation. She insisted that she would be furious if this was not resolved.

So you see, Michael, friction does not go away, and yet it is so painful with hindsight to see what one could have done and how one could have avoided something. But the bottom line is that we do not have the luxury of hindsight in the moment, and our machines or even Souls can only do what they can do. It is useless to say criminal and wring our hands. Right work is to see it, bear it, try

165

and avoid it again if you can and remember it was not you, but what you are observing.

It is always a temptation to blame oneself and become defeated by judgement. If we sin we sin. If our mechanics attract certain friction and we observe and work and remove what caused us to stumble, do you really think you would have removed friction forever? Even now, Michael, I try and keep learning by my failings, and the higher one goes, the greater and more poignant the friction. I do not know if we can become good enough or perfect enough to avoid friction, so do not run yourself down so badly. When you find an inequity or sin or feature, see it, remove what you can, and move on. You will have the opportunity to have another go – I promise.

Sometimes people think that to be conscious means to be perfect. No, it means to be Conscious. Conscious to the madness, the treachery, the crime and hate produced by man, Conscious to the great laws, Michael. To see the lower consuming the higher is terrifying and one has to be Conscious of and to it. Conscious as one looks into the face of a crying child and Conscious to former friends devouring one and one's life's work like a pack of rabid dogs. Conscious that "they do not know what they do." And Conscious to one's death.

These are the things you must learn to swallow, Michael, and seeing one's own mechanics or features and how awfully they manifest are but a prelude to the awakening journey.

Endure, Michael. Endure.

To be Awake means that one will see things as they really are, not as in a dream. Angels must survive and prevail here – that bears testimony to the fact that so few of us endure the whole journey.

Perhaps you felt that when you awaken you will have no mechanics. You always will, but can you make them in their lunacy serve your Soul and your wish to live?

These are the preparations we need to live in higher worlds. A man who lives in a higher world can observe how now it is not the I's* but people, who try and put him to sleep or prevent his soul from awakening. Now you are in a world of your own I's, but one day, those inner conflicts and will become people with cunning and intelligence.

Right now you look on your mechanics as a curse, but one day it may save your life.

Hold on, Michael. Hold on.

I look forward to serving you more.

Love,
Mervyn

---

* I's refers to all the thoughts, feelings and impulses that we generate. Mistakenly, we entertain each of these voices as I: I'd like a cheeseburger, I think he thinks I'm stupid, I wish that car would hurry up, etc. By virtue of having a body, we will always have these conversations, but we are much more than these thoughts and impulse, these I's. The Real I is the Soul.

9
THE LOVE STUFF

There is a huge difference between love and the object or person that stimulates the love. One is a state that can be preserved, while the other can manifest in many ways.

The highest ideal must be teaching people how to give and receive love; Love that puts body, heart and soul in harmony.

Awaken your heart and the thaw comes ...

The birth of Venus shows the love that is inside us without the identification with the object of love.

Awakening love and experiencing God are one and the same.
The more awake you become, the more you have to love.

The object of the love, or the lover, awakens the love that is already inside of us.

We were designed TO love, not to BE loved.
And that is why if an enemy hates you, and you love him.

(You are in a STATE OF LOVE)
The stronger the enemy is,
the stronger that love can become.

You see, that is very different
from what we think of as ROMANTIC LOVE --
meeting someone and holding hands
and living in a cottage 'til we are old.

Love pours OUT of us ... That's the next revelation.
It doesn't flow INTO us.

We think, "I need love."
No you don't!

It is:"I need TO love."

--Excerpts from Online Meetings, 2000 and Lecture in NYC,
"Evolution of Love, Relationships, & the Soul," 2006.

THE HOSPITAL

Nothing prepared me for the next stage of my life, a release of hormones that would forever destroy the innocent child and send me reeling for the rest of my life. Mother Nature snuck up on me and really did a number on me.

I was eleven-years-old and weighed about 165lbs. But I didn't have a real problem with this; by then I had basically overcome most of the cruelty that my peers dished out. There wasn't an insult I hadn't heard, and I thought I was prepared for anything that had to do with my fatness. So it took me by surprise when one day my mother announced that she was taking me to Jervis Street hospital to check out my weight. The only time I had been to a hospital was when I was a lot younger, visiting my father. I immediately learned to hate that awful hospital smell and wasn't in any hurry to go back. Anyway, the doctors told my mum that they wanted me in the hospital for a few weeks for tests and things. And this is how my great adventure began.

Ma asked Brother Coleman to excuse me from school, explaining that I had to go to hospital for a few weeks. I remember Brother Coleman being surprisingly kind and sympathetic. I arrived at the hospital with my mum, holding a little bag with my new pajamas. This was my first new pair of pajamas. We couldn't afford them, but now I had to have them. In fact, I had two pairs, so one could be washed while the other was being worn. Jesus, that was extravagance!

A lovely blonde nurse introduced herself as "Pamela." After she put the screens around my bed, she told me to get into my pajamas and then into bed.

"But it's only two in the afternoon," I protested. She smiled and told me that these were the rules.

Ma kissed me goodbye and said she would visit me tomorrow. As she waved and vanished behind the curtains, I suddenly felt so alone. My mother stood between me and the great abyss of life and the unknown; without her I was very small, vulnerable and afraid. I held back a tear as I studied this strange place around me. I had no idea what they were going to do to me or if it would hurt. Then I heard Harry's words in my head, "They're going to have to cut the fat off ya, or else they're going to put ya in a room that's real hot so you sweat for weeks until ya shrink."

So I lay there, sweating about all the terrible things that could happen. Thank God Nurse Pam interrupted my thoughts when she came by to remove the screens, revealing what would be my home for the next couple of weeks. I was in a big ward with twelve beds – six on each side, a very high ceiling and a big Georgian window with twelve frames. Maybe that meant there was a window for each person. The man in the bed on my left was Duffy and the man on my right was Val. I liked Val immediately. He asked me how old I was. When he heard I was only eleven, he called the nurse over and told her that I should be in the children's ward, not a ward for very sick men. Nurse Pam explained that because

I wasn't really sick, I couldn't go to the children's ward and besides, this was the only place they could find a bed for me. Many years later, I learned that this kind of circular thinking is "Irish logic."

At six o'clock they brought around dinner. It was lovely and you got a great pudding as well. Maybe it was the pudding, but for the first time I felt that things weren't going to be so bad – I might even have a pretty good time. At nine, it was lights out and everyone went to sleep. I lay in the dark, feeling the clean starched sheets and enjoying a whole bed to myself. I looked around feeling the darkness and solitude closing in on me. Then, in the distance, I heard the most beautiful music: the most holy hymn sung by a choir of angels. It started gently, slowly, and began to get louder and closer. It was really sad and made me cry, not because I was sad, but because it was so beautiful and I knew God was very near. Harry told me that you can't see God if you're in a body, but you can know when he is near.

That beautiful smell of roses, and that familiar feeling of lightness and floating, told me that God was near. I asked, through my tears, why I was fat and in hospital. Although I couldn't see God, I knew he was smiling just like me ma when I asked her a stupid question. He never answers, but I always know that he hears me and that everything is okay. This sounds kind of stupid, but I know in these moments that I'll never die and that for some reason I have to be brave and take on this life. The music was so beautiful that it lifted me up and up until I was the music, the breeze and even the smell of the hospital. I heard the rise and fall of my own breath and the black night wrapped around me like warm blanket.

I awoke, abruptly, at two in the morning, to Duffy roaring in pain. I was frightened, then relieved, to see two nurses running in and putting screens around him. He must have been howling for a couple of hours. I'd heard the children at school howling in pain from the cane and the strap, but nothing prepared me for Duffy's howling. I didn't think that pain could extract that kind of sound from a grown man.

I remember thinking how strange we were. One minute, I'm feeling sorry for old Duffy, the next minute, I'm angry with him for keeping me awake. And then I'm feeling sorry for myself in case I had what Duffy had. I finally got back to sleep despite the commotion going on beside me.

The next morning at 7:30, I woke to the clang of a bell. A little Dublin lady was standing over me with a tray asking me if I wanted breakfast.

"Two soft boiled eggs and toast, no butter. Tea or coffee?"

I never had coffee in my life, sure, that was something only Tony Caffola and the Italians drank.

"Tea," I said, sitting up to make soldiers out of my toast.

"Wait a minute," I said, "I can't eat toast without butter."

"Sorry, darling. It says here under no circumstances are

you to get any butter. Don't ask me, I'm just doing my job," she replied.

It was then I noticed that Duffy was gone.

"Where's Duffy?"

Val told me he died during the night, and I nearly jumped out of bed in shock and fright. How could I be dunking toast soldiers in my egg when, only a few hours ago, Duffy died, right next to me? My mind raced and thought of God, death, living; and then I continued eating my breakfast. Thank God for the needs of the body because sometimes it stops you from going stark raving mad.

Val called the nurse to complain about me having to see a man die. She answered him in a way that only an Irish country girl could answer.

"Sure, listen now, Val, it'll do him no harm at all to see a man die. Sure, it wasn't as if it was himself that was dying now, was it?"

"Yeah, but he's only a kid."

"Sure, your man's not a kid, Val. Sure, look at the size of him, he's bigger than me own father."

Val looked up at her as she came around the side of his bed. I saw his hand going up the back of her uniform. She let him for a minute, then smiled and pulled away.

"Stop it, Val. That young fella is looking."

Jesus! I couldn't believe this. One minute I'm old enough to see old Duffy die, and the next I'm too young to see a bit of affection going on between the nurse and her patient.

"So you're Mervyn and why are you here?" The nurse asked as she came over and picked up my chart.

"I don't know. I think it's because I'm fat."

"Sure, you're a fine lump of a lad. We'll soon sort you out. Have you done a motion today?"

"Well, I've turned around a few times and sat up and had breakfast?"

"No, silly, I don't mean that kind of a motion," she laughed. "I mean, have you had a bowel movement?"

I didn't, for the life of me, know if my bowels had moved or not. I mean, how do you know? "I don't really know," I said quietly.

The more she laughed, the more mortified I became. She was now looking at me like I was a moron.

"I don't know what you mean," I said weakly.
She looked at me in that strange way that people have looked at me all my life - as if I fell out of the sky from another planet.

"Did you do a number one or a number two today?" She asked.

"No," I replied.

Then I knew what she was talking about. I remembered our conversation with the lads; maybe Derrick Shannon was right, sex was connected to going to the toilet in front of a girl. I felt my face turn red. Why on earth would she want to know that?

When she moved off to another bed, I asked Val if he was using that butter on his plate. He passed it over to me.

Now, I had a lovely breakfast. Imagine not giving me any butter?

After a couple days there I realized that it was okay, they ask you about your motions all the time. Although whenever Nurse Pam would ask me I'd blush and I didn't know why. But she smelled nice, and I got a funny feeling in my belly.

That evening my mother and one of my sisters visited, bringing me fruit and some comics. I cried while telling her about Duffy, and she said she would pray for him. I sometimes used to think God was angry with Ireland, the entire country. Imagine every day all those begging prayers, I mean, God killed Duffy, didn't He? So what was the point of praying to God for him? People would pray for a new baby, a broken leg, a drunk's Soul and the hussy next door. I mean, I would get angry if I were God. I would remind them all that it was me that did it in the first place.

Me ma smiled at me and told me that God came for Duffy in the night, taking him because He loved him. This really confused me because it seemed to me that Duffy must have not loved God, because he sure as hell didn't want to go with Him. He roared for hours. Why would he do that if God, who loved him, was calling him. Then a horrible thought crossed my mind. Sweet Jesus! What if it wasn't God who came for him? What if it was the devil himself?

I looked over at the empty bed and suddenly felt nauseous with the thought that the devil had been there, just a few hours before. I fell back on my pillow.

"Jesus, Mary and Joseph!" my mother cried. "What the hell's happened to you? You're white as a sheet!"

I couldn't say anything. God had visited me earlier. I remembered hearing that beautiful music from the angels. Then only an hour or two later, the devil himself came for Duffy. Jesus! You couldn't come into hospital sick without one or the other coming for you.

I asked me ma if the devil could come for you. She answered that of course he could, but that you had to be really wicked. She didn't know the devil had taken Duffy. What, in the name of God, must have Duffy done to deserve such a terrible fate? Everyone who came by, even the priest, was praying for him, up in heaven. I was the only one who knew he wasn't there. Then I realized we never pray for the Souls in hell because we think they're all in heaven. I would be the only one who prayed for Duffy in hell. I was the only hope the poor guy had.

I still had to explain why I had gone white, so I asked me ma if they were really going to cut my fat off like Harry had said. She laughed at me the way God did the night before telling me not to be stupid. If it's stupid not to know and stupid to ask, I was doomed to be stupid.

Anyway, she told me three of my friends were outside and she had to leave. Those days they only let three people in at a time. We looked at each other without saying a word. We often did that; we would say with our eyes the things that we didn't know how to say, sharing a connection that we didn't quite understand. All I knew was that when we did this, I always felt happy and sad and missed me ma, even when she was there, right in front of me.

We waved goodbye, and I knew I was in for another night of visitations.

A moment later, down at the end of the ward, I heard my mother shouting at Harry and telling him off for terrifying me about my fat getting cut off. When the boys finally arrived at my section, they looked look like scared, lost sheep. None of them had ever been in such a big building, much less a hospital, before. When they spotted me in bed, they were shocked.

"What's the matter with you, Fatser?" they asked, concerned and curious. "Are you sick?"

"No, I'm too fucken' big for my age and they just want to slow down how much I'm growing." I was amazed how quickly my brain could invent such a good story. I congratulated myself.

I looked at Harry, but he didn't say a word. He never did if it appeared he was in the wrong. I told them about Duffy. They loved hearing anything about death.

"Did ya see a black or a white angel coming for him?" Derek wanted to know.

"Fucken' screens were around, so how in the name of Jesus was I supposed to see?" I snapped, a little harder than I meant. I didn't want to tell them about the devil coming for

Duffy.

They brought me more comics and lots of sweets and chocolates from all the boys in the class. This hospital business was going to be a good thing with all these goodies and attention. There was also something great about meeting the boys here; because they were familiar, they took away the strangeness of the hospital. I really felt like my friends were a part of me, more than I ever did hanging around with them in the neighborhood. They laughed when I asked them if they knew what a motion was. They laughed even harder when I told them that it was a bowel movement. Then Harry said that meant that a fart was an air movement. We cracked up some more and told more jokes. But every now and then I caught them looking at Duffy's empty bed. When they left, I knew they were wondering if I would be next.

As soon as they were out of sight, another nurse, called Shirley, appeared by my side and went through my booty. She separated all the sweets from the fruit and told me that all the sweets were going down to the poor children in the children's ward.

"Wait a minute, I'm poor, too!" I tried to reason. But she explained that it was the doctor's order that I wasn't to have any sweets. She gave me a peck on the cheek and took off with my stuff, leaving me with four bloody apples.

At least I found a way to get butter with my next morning's breakfast. Val didn't like butter and gave me his, an arrangement that lasted for a while - until the nurses caught on. I was getting bored lying in bed, so I asked Nurse Eileen if I could wander around. At lunch, a little Dublin woman came by, pushing a big trolley of food and trays. Out of sheer boredom I offered to help her.

She was so typical of a type of Dublin woman in the catering and domestic trades. They were all really old and wore horrid, old, ill-fitting shoes with nylons that hung down their varicose-veined legs. They'd chew with their gums because their heads had shrunk and their false teeth didn't fit properly anymore. One eye would be nearly shut closed from spending years with a fag hanging out of the side of their mouths. But they had a heart of gold. You just knew they were somebody's mother and that they had no false illusions about life. They were always giving advice. Her name was Peggy. She'd gasp a lot, being short of breath. And I often wondered why she wouldn't take the fag out of her mouth. In those days, you could smoke anywhere, but it wasn't considered nice if you let any fag-ash fall onto the food.

I spent a lot of time helping her. Sometimes we came across old people who were really sick. They frightened me, so I didn't look at them in the eyes. It made me glad that I was a kid. It must be awful, lying in the bed, wondering if God or the devil were coming for you. After a few days of sorting them out, I knew who was going to hell and who was going to heaven. I was surprised to find that most of them were going to hell. People who smiled at me were definitely going to heaven, and all the old grumpy fuckers were off to grumpyland. I mean, you couldn't have grumpy old fuckers in heaven, could you? One good thing about the grumpy ones was that, more often than not, they'd wave you away when you brought them their meals. Jesus, you'd think you were offering them a bowl of shite.

Five days later, the doctors appeared when me ma was visiting me. They were concerned that I had put on five pounds in weight since I entered the hospital, despite my strict diet. My mum told me they wanted to do blood tests and to check other things they hadn't done yet. She also told me not to worry because the doctors were great and would sort me out. My mother thought doctors were gods. If they wanted to cut off my fucken' leg, she'd have thanked them and told me off if I complained. She loved gentlemen and educated people, and doctors were both.

That evening Nurse Pam was on duty. She came by when the lights went out. In a soft, conspiratorial whisper, she asked me how I put on five pounds. I confessed how much I loved pudding. And I earnestly explained that I only ate the pudding from the patients that didn't want them when I was helping old Peggy. She laughed sweetly and gave me a big hug.

Once again, I was foiled. I was banned from helping old Peggy with the food trays.

I didn't know I was doing anything wrong. Nobody had told me that it was bad to eat as much pudding as I liked. Up to that point in my life I could eat my fill, no guilt, no shame; now, those days were over.

Val couldn't get out of bed, so a nurse would routinely come by with a trolley of soapy water and towels to give him a sponge bath. I'd never heard of this before, but I suppose it made sense. Anyway, one morning Nurse Pam asked if I would like a sponge bath. She put up the screens around my bed before I could say "no." I was rolled over and my pajamas were pulled down before I could object. While my bum was washed like a baby's, I had the strangest feelings. She turned me over to wash between my legs with warm soapy water, and now that strange feeling was getting stronger. When she dried me with a towel, I was mortified because my mickey had grown. That had happened before, but nothing like this. I saw that she saw it, and she saw that I saw that she saw it, and our eyes met.

There was all this silent stuff that went on when I looked in me ma's eyes. But this was different; this was much more powerful. It nearly took my breath away. I had fallen in love. Nurse Pam wasn't just a nurse; she was a beautiful Goddess.

After she packed up her stuff and left, I lay there with love pouring out of me. I was going to marry her and live happy ever after. I'd never felt like this before and my mickey took on a life of its own again. I touched it and that lovely feeling ran right through me, so I touched it again and again. Something wonderful was happening - was this love or what? The feeling in my stomach was reaching an urgency that I didn't understand, so I kept touching myself. Then it started. An amazing exquisite rush came out of me. I was breathless as warm, sticky stuff shot out of me, all over my hands. I was in heaven.

I don't know how long I floated off, thinking of Pam and touching myself, when suddenly I fell back to earth with a disturbing thought. Sweet Jesus! What was this sticky stuff all over my hands? Then the horror: I knew why I was here in the hospital; I was infected inside. Like a boil, I had just exploded!

I was dying, rotting from the inside. And they wouldn't tell me because they knew I couldn't handle it. Oh God! Maybe that's what Duffy died from, too. Maybe tonight was going to be my night. I lay very still on my bed, saying goodbye to my mother, father, sisters, brother and everyone else. I was going to die, alone, in a hospital bed. I needed to see a priest and say my confession. Tears rolled down my cheeks as I waited for death. Would it be God or the devil, coming for me?

How could I have been so stupid, thinking I was here for no reason? Then I began thinking of Pam again, her lovely smile and her lovely smell, and I started touching myself again. The lovely feeling started to grow again as I imagined Pam in her knickers. Was I going mad? I was in my last hours on earth, and all I was thinking about was lovely Nurse Pam in her lovely drawers. But the feeling kept growing to a mad frenzy until I was squirting more and more puss all over my hands. Heaven...bliss...again. A few seconds later, I was thinking straight, again. My hands were sticky and I felt like a dirty bastard. What was going on?

I stared at the ceiling thinking all sorts of thoughts like a condemned man. Then I reasoned that if I was full of puss I'd better get it all out. Thus began a night of therapy, "therapy" that would last through my whole life. Something inside was unleashed, and every time it was released, I felt better. That night came and went very fast. I was so busy that I completely forgot about God or the devil. By morning, I concluded that since I was still alive I must be curing myself, so I spent all the next day and night getting all the puss out.

I was getting really good at "curing" myself. I also noticed that my thoughts about Pam were getting filthier and filthier. But, to my relief, I noted that I didn't think about her going to the toilet - maybe Harry was wrong after all.

Nurse Pam must have seen the love I was developing for her. Every time she came by, I smiled like a real eegit and said stupid things like, "You're the best nurse I ever met in my life" or "All my life I wanted to be a nurse like you." Then on the third day, I started imagining Nurse Eileen in her knickers. That evening, I was even thinking of Val putting his big hand up the big country nurse's skirt. On the fourth day, I imagined old Peggy in her knickers, and I got the wrong kind of bad pain in my crotch. I was learning that you had to think the girl – or at least a part of her – was beautiful. Peggy's varicose veins didn't work.

On a larger scale, now that they had stopped my innocent food gathering, I was losing weight. One evening the doctor announced that he was very pleased with my progress. We didn't talk about the puss thing, but I knew what he meant.

Now, I was falling in love with Rosie from the laundry room. I'd frequently visit the laundry room to chat with the women working there. I had met them in the canteen one day, and they had invited me to come by. Rosie had real clean, white shoes and tanned legs, and she looked at me in a way that reminded me of Nurse Pam. That was enough to get me down there. She'd look at me and smile while she was emptying the big laundry baskets. I was in love again.

I went down to visit her every day until one day she asked me how old I was. When I said "eleven," she exclaimed, "Jesus, Mary and Joseph! I thought you were sixteen 'cause you're in the men's ward. You're a fucken' baby!"

I suppose I was bigger than most boys my age, and I guess I looked older than eleven. I slinked back to the ward feeling like a rejected puppy. I think that was my first real rejection. I went back to my bed and cried. What was wrong with being only eleven anyway? Nobody had told me about the puss, my feelings or hormones. I went into hospital to get "sorted out," and I did. I went in a child and came out a budding man.

For weeks after I left the hospital, I kept my secret and kept on drawing out the "puss." I didn't even tell Harry.

But as the weeks passed, I started understanding things and I finally figured out that this is the stuff that makes babies. A quick check through an old encyclopedia informed me that there were five million babies shot out every time you did that. Jesus Christ! That meant I was killing babies by the millions! That night I struggled with mass genocide. The equivalent of the entire human race was wiped out on my sheets. Then I understood how God doesn't really mean it when he kills off loads of people.

Many weeks later, on a Saturday morning, I walked slowly down the stairs and overheard my mother talking to my big sister. I know she was talking loud enough so I would hear.

"I'm going to have to talk to Father Murphy about that big fella," she said.

I froze in terror on the stairs. To be reported to the priest was the ultimate punishment.

"I don't know what the hell goes on in that bed of his, but there's all this disgusting stuff all over the sheets. I'm going to ask the Father what's going on."

I ran back upstairs in terror thinking, "Oh my God, my mother knows and my sister and now Father Murphy is going to know!" I wanted to drop dead. I swore to God that I would never do it again. Then I flinched again. Was this a sin? Nobody ever mentioned it, perhaps it wasn't, or maybe I'd invented a new sin. Jesus, that meant I'd have to confess this at Confession.

That night before bed, I negotiated with God and we agreed that neither of us would mention it again. I told him that if it was a sin, I was very sorry, but I couldn't stop and there's no way I was ever going to confess that to Father Murphy. I would gladly burn in hell for eternity than tell him. I think I worked that one out through sheer fear, but I couldn't quite reconcile killing all the babies. That was the sin that lay heavy on my Soul. I was a Catholic boy, sinning right in front of God himself: committing genocide several times a day and refusing to confess this to a priest. To this day, I'm not sure whether it ruined me or gave me character for standing up to God.

Weeks later when I was at Harry's laughing and messing around I heard the word "wank" for the first time. Harry did it again; he explained everything and made everything right. I was overjoyed. I was normal. Then he dropped the bomb:

"It makes you go blind."

THE GIRLS

Harry knocked on my door all excited. He could hardly contain himself and wouldn't tell me why until we were well out of my mother's earshot.

"Did you see that new young one from England over in O'Reilly's house?"

He meant Kathy O'Reilly from across the road. She had cousins in England, and we knew two of them were coming to Dublin for the summer holidays. He told me he was in love with the one of them, Amanda.

"And listen, Fatser, you can have the sister, she's Bonny."

A strange feeling came over me, a feeling I didn't have a word for. In the back of my mind I wondered what exactly we were going to do with them once we had them.

We practically ran to Kathy's house and knocked on her door. A tall girl with long, black hair opened the door. She had a nice smile. She looked at Harry and said "allo."

I never heard anyone say hello like that before so I knew she was one of the English ones. I looked over at Harry. I didn't know it then, but I was witnessing the great demise of the great Harry. I never saw him like that before - red faced and embarrassed.

They stared at each other for a long time. Then he asked, stammering, if Kathy was in. I couldn't understand what had happened. Some strange signal was passed, recognized and understood, all in seconds. I had witnessed the arrival of a new force that plunged into the two of them. It was so powerful that I felt it – and it's still burned somewhere deep inside me. She was a nice girl, in fact, she reminded me of meself. I remembered thinking that that kind of made sense because Harry liked me too, as a friend, as well.

"Kathy! There's two blokes out here for you."

Blokes? We were blokes! I didn't know the word. But I loved the way she said it.

Kathy came out and officially introduced Amanda. She said "allo" to me, but I saw she only had eyes for Harry. I waited for "mine" to come out, but Kathy said Bonny was sleeping and would see us later.

We left the house. Harry wasn't Harry any more, he was acting all funny. He picked a little flower from the garden, smelled it and smiled in a stupid way. He offered me the flower to smell, and I told him to fuck off. He looked at me, surprised, as if I was common and told me that I had to learn to appreciate the little things in life. I told him to fuck off again, and he just ignored me.

"I loved the way she talked," I said.

He raised the flower to his face again as we walked into my garden. He slowly sat down on the grass and gazed at the sky. I knew he wasn't really looking at the sky.

"Fatser, do you believe in fate?" he asked me in a real sincere voice. In fact he almost whispered it.

"Of course I believe in faith; I'm a Catholic, aren't I?" I said that because I didn't know what "fate" meant then. "And, anyway, how can you believe in faith when it's believing? I believe in God and I have faith in him."

Harry wasn't listening to me. He had a handful of grass and dropped it from his hand, watching it catch the wind as if it was first time he ever saw grass. Impatiently, I asked him if he was all right. He didn't answer. He just sat there as I stared at him. Then I finally understood what was happening. He was "experiencing the roses" just like I used to at Stephen's Green, only this time he was "experiencing" the grass. Now that I knew what was happening, I sat quietly with him and "experienced" the flowers in the garden.

We both sat there, experiencing, for ages. We would sigh softly, and I tried experiencing the grass, as well. It worked. I saw all the leaves of grass. I saw how each one was an individual just like me, Harry, and all the fellas. I even started to think real funny things like, how does the grass know when to stop growing? How does it know how to suck up the water from the ground?

Harry looked at me and sighed. He told me I was the most understanding friend he ever had. We looked into each other's eyes deeply for a few seconds. When I thought he was going to kiss me, I got a little spooked and stopped "experiencing" immediately.

"Jesus, Harry! What's gotten into you?"

He just smiled and said he thought he was falling in

love.

For a terrible second I thought he meant he was falling in love with me. Then I remembered Amanda. And then I understood that "experiencing" and falling in love are very similar. I also noted that it took an Amanda to make Harry "experience." Perhaps when people fall in love they release all their magic powers.

Until now, I thought I was the only one who could experience. Now, my best friend Harry was doing it. From here on, there would be so much more we could share. I told Harry it was great to see him like this, and he nodded knowingly at me. We looked into each other's eyes like two eejits in love, gazing at each other for the first time. We were drunk on something - he on Amanda and me on flowers. I floated a little higher when I understood that men give women flowers to make them feel like this. Then we slowly said good bye and went home for our tea. I turned around to watch Harry walk up the road. He was moving in slow motion, like he was in a dream. He slowly, ever so gently, kicked a stone and watched patiently to see where it rolled.

My father was in a foul mood when he came home that evening and wouldn't let me out of the house. I begged and bargained with everything in my power, but nothing worked and I was sent to bed for my cheek.

Defeated, I looked out my bedroom window and saw the fellas standing on the corner talking to the girls. I saw

Harry and Amanda off to one side. There was a blonde girl that I didn't recognize. Could that be Bonny?

I plopped in bed and cursed my father. It wasn't fair that I should be in bed just because of him. He was a law that I wanted to be free from, but I had no idea how to do that yet. I mean, how do you get rid of your own da when he's always breathing down your neck?

Next morning I asked Harry how it went. Jesus, he still had that stupid smile on his face. Where was the hard Harry that all the fellas feared? He had turned into a sucker overnight.

"I kissed her, Fatser."

That was better than anything I had expected.

Tell me what happened?" I wanted to know everything. I'd only dreamed of what it would be like to kiss a girl.

"She gave me an incredible french kiss," he sighed.

"But she's English? Isn't she?" I asked puzzled.

Harry looked at me like he was looking at a first rate eegit, and laughed.

"Don't tell me you don't know what a french kiss is?" Then he explained it the way only Harry could.

I wasn't too sure if I liked the sound of what he described. I mean why on God's green earth would a girl want to stick her tongue down your throat? And why would you want to do that back?

It was all the talk in the playground that day. Harry had French-kissed Amanda. Derek asked me if I had heard that Harry was sticking his tongue in Amanda's ear all night, and that she was teaching him French? Then Patsy explained that french kissing was when you tried to rub that little thing that hangs down at the back of your throat with your tongue. That was supposed to drive the women crazy.

The rumors were flying in all directions. But there was one thing that was certain; Harry was the hero of the day. He'd been the first one into the breach, and we all wanted to be part of it. Fellas, even from other classes, were coming over to talk to a beaming Harry who was all too delighted to retell his story. A crowd of lads gathering around him, imagining a french kiss. A couple fellas grimaced, and a few spit hard as if they had just eaten something awful.

One of the bigger fellas told Harry he was full of shite because he was in France last year on his holidays and that wasn't how French girls kiss. Twenty of us lads looked at him in amazement. We asked him how he knew and if he did know that, then how did they kiss? He turned beet red, muttering that we were all sick bastards and to fuck off.

Harry was radiating some kind of weird energy, infecting us. We were all like headless chickens, eager to understand, eager to earn our spurs. Something new was entering our blood. We were changing and life would never be the same again.

Later, I mentioned this to my older sister, and she called

Amanda an "English slut."

"They're all sluts over in England. They go around naked under their clothes and kiss anybody…. They're all tarts."

Although I pretended to be shocked, this was really good news because now it was virtually guaranteed that I was going to get to do some unholy things with Bonny. My sister told me English girls are after only one thing, only she didn't tell me what that was. But I figured it was going to be something good.

Word spread that Kathy's parents were going away for the weekend and she was throwing a party. We were all surprised because it was nobody's birthday, but Harry cleared up the confusion. He explained that it was going to be a party like the ones they had in London… the English girls were going to show us "English games."

Yes, something big was happening, and we were all changing.

The next day Harry told me he was taking Amanda down to the Memorial Park and then for a walk along the River Liffey. He wanted me to come along to keep Bonny company. So after school, I met Harry and we went to collect the girls. While we were waiting for them, I started getting really excited. We were only going for a walk, but I felt like I was going on my first date. I noticed that I was walking kind of funny and standing against the railings like an American cowboy. I wondered why my body was doing that. Why was I walking like Roy Rogers? Harry was doing it too, because every now and then Harry and I would stop and spit real far.

Bonny was two years older than me. She had long curly blonde hair and big blue eyes that were very far apart. She looked like she was "experiencing" just by being alive. She smiled and looked really friendly. I was relieved, too, when she didn't remind me I was fat.

I noticed her voice. She talked lovely, real gentle, like she had just woken up from a long nap. She shook my hand.

"It's weely nithe to meet you, Merwin."

My God, she had an adowable (sorry, adorable) lisp.

It seemed her tongue was a bit too big to fit in her mouth because you'd see it a lot when you looked at her. She thought everything was a real scream and when she laughed, she laughed really loud. She had a big mouth and you could see far down her throat. She had a Santa Claus nose that didn't match the rest of her. She was like an angel, and she seemed completely unaware of all the dirty thoughts that were going through my head. It made me feel a little bit guilty.

She was wearing a simple white dress and holding an enormous bag of sandwiches for the picnic. She asked me if I liked "pop" and I told her of course I did, even though I didn't have a clue what it was. Harry had said he liked "pop", so I knew I was all right.

As we set off down the road, I couldn't help but notice

there was a gang of the lads standing on the corner watching us. We pretended we didn't see them. It was a two mile walk to the park, and on the way I noticed that Bonny kind of believed everything I said. She kept saying "wow" to everything I said, so I kept saying things.

"Does your uncle really have race horses?" she asked, wide-eyed with excitement.

"Thirty-two of them," I lied. I could have sworn she moved closer to me because of that. She told me I had lovely eyes and asked when she could see the horses.

Harry and Amanda were oblivious to us. When we got to a quiet spot overlooking the river, they stretched out in the grass and started kissing. I looked at the french kissing they were doing with great interest. It looked like they were sucking the same sweet and trying to get it out of each other's mouth. Harry was kind of moaning and so was Amanda.

Bonny and I looked at each other, pretending that we sat by this kind of thing every day. Bonny broke the silence of the heavy breathing by telling me that she really hurt her hip on the ship coming over from England.

"Do you want to see?" she asked as she hiked her skirt right past the top of her knickers.

I was gobsmacked. This was better than anything I could have dreamed. I was looking at the most gorgeous thing ever - a beautiful, medium-sized bruise on the side of her beautiful hip. A massive rush of energy plunged into me and filled me with electricity. I was kind of trembling, weak and breathless.

"Oh, you poor thing!" I squealed. "Sure, you have a terrible bruise on your little hip."

"Have I weely?" she said, looking very worried and standing up so she could get a better look. "Where is it?"

I reached over and pulled her knickers to one side, but she still couldn't see it. I couldn't believe my luck, she must have been the stupidest girl on God's good green earth or she was just playing with me. She responded to every concern I showed and even bent over so I could examine the bruise better. I'd never felt or seen anything like this in my life. Her skin was so much nicer than Harry's or mine. In front of me was everything I had fantasized since that day in the hospital.

Well, right then, Harry opened his eyes and saw us. Good ole Fatser, rubbing a cute girl's bare arse. Harry's dumbfounded expression said it all: He couldn't believe that all he was getting was just a kiss, and here was Fatser with a girl's skirt up in the air.

We continued our hike. But just to rub it in, every few hundred yards or so, I'd whisper to Bonny that I wanted to check her bruise again. So, of course, whenever Harry looked back, he'd see me with Bonny against a tree – with her skirt hiked up.

I felt like I was back at the hospital again. That incredible energy was back, and now it was because of Bonny. It didn't occur to me to do anything except to examine her bum and worship her. I started to "experience" in a big way, although,

I knew I wasn't falling in love, the way Harry and Amanda were.

Bonny was amazed by everything I said. I showed her sheep and she was excited. I showed her trees and explained how birds make nests, and she was thrilled. When I climbed up a tree and brought her a sparrow's egg, she had tears in her eyes as she kissed the little egg. God, I'd never seen such lovely softness. I'd never seen sweetness over an egg. We normally threw the eggs in the bushes. She was horrified when I made this suggestion and made me climb back up and put the egg back in the nest.

Then I caught Harry and Amanda going into the bushes. I was about to follow them when Harry turned around and shot me a dirty look. I got the message. Bonny and I sat on the grass. Now that the excitement of having seen her knickers had passed a bit, my body wanted more – of what, I wasn't sure.

In 1958 Ireland, there was strict censorship. We had never seen a pair of breasts or had any idea what sex was. All we had were our basic instincts and rumors. We had no idea what to do with a girl, so everything that was circulating in me was pure chemistry, without thoughts or words.

Bonny stretched out her legs and lay back on her elbows. She looked at me in a way that made me blush and feel really stupid at the same time. I knew I was supposed to do something and that she was expecting me to do something, but I didn't have a clue what to do.

I was sitting closer to Bonny than I ever had to any other girl in my life. She smelled wonderful. I wanted to stick my nose in her hair and keep smelling her deeply. The other Mervyn, in my head, immediately went berserk, shouting that I was crazy. "Look at you, you stupid eejit, a beautiful girl wanting you, and all you want to do is SMELL her?"

She looked into my eyes and I saw her, I mean, I think I saw her Soul. We looked at each other for a long moment and then she spoke very softly.

"You're a weely nice person Merwin." She reached out and stroked my hair.

God, it was like I had been touched by the Virgin Mary herself. I was nearly in a swoon. The only other person who touched my hair was my mother and Brother Coleman – to pull it. At last, someone saw me and understood me. I was shocked at the way my body and mind reacted to this tender act. I felt like a little puppy squirming in joy. If I had a tail I would have wagged it. Jesus Christ, then I remembered all my lies. What was I going to tell her when she wanted to see my uncle's non-existent horses? I was swooning one moment and mortified with embarrassment the next.

Eventually, Harry and Amanda appeared. They were both pink and kept staring at the ground. They must have done something really awful or really great because I saw guilt all over their faces. We walked silently along the river, each of us quietly digesting everything, when Bonny starting shouting and pointing.

"Look, look woewers!"

I ran up to where she was and saw rowers from the rowing club out on the river. We stood there watching them for a while, as I wondered how you become a rower. We'd see these fellas from the Ballyfermot side of the river. They probably had loads of money and posh fathers. Sometimes we'd ambush them as they came around the bend in the river. We'd hide in trees, fling sticks and stones at them, and then run like the clappers. Somehow we felt we were getting even with something.

Then Amanda said we had to be getting home, so we started the trek back. I noticed that I was never the one to suggest when we come or go. I silently told myself that one day I would be the one to suddenly say, "let's go."

Bonny kissed me on the cheek and told me she was looking forward to seeing me at the party the next day.

After Harry and I left the girls, we headed to Harry's garden for a chat to reflect on the day's events. The far end of Harry's garden was the only place we had absolute privacy, and if someone was coming, we could spot them first.

I didn't like to keep secrets from Harry because we told each other everything, so I told him the truth about Bonny and the bruise.

"Fatser you're a right bastard," he roared laughing. "How could you do that to the poor girl?"

I was shocked by his reaction, especially because I

knew, given half the chance, he would have done the exact same thing. Then I realized he'd probably never be in that situation with a girl because he was too rough, and Bonny wouldn't have trusted him anyway. With that thought, St. Mervyn's voice thundered in my head, reminding me that Bonny trusted me, and pointing out how I sinned and what a dirty little bastard I was.

Harry had done it again. He was right when I knew he was wrong. But why did his being right always made me feel bad and stupid. This was a phenomenon that would take me thirty years to figure out. How was Harry always right? How did he always know what was right and wrong? Was he secretly taking lessons? I thought I was good, but apparently I wasn't. I suffered these thoughts for a while. Then I asked Harry how he got on with Amanda.

"Jesus, Fatser. Your sister is right about those English girls."

He looked around the garden to make sure that nobody was around. I knew this was going to be good, but nothing could have prepared me for what Harry was about to tell me. Harry lowered his voice and told me that when they went into the bushes, Amanda was really excited - she started kissing him really hard and was moaning a lot. Then she looked at Harry and told him she wanted to give him a "blow job."

"What's a 'blow job'?" I asked, confused.

"Shut up, Fatser, and let me tell you, for God's sake."

Then he checked the garden again.

"She knelt down in front of me and opened my fly and took my mickey out."

"And did she blow on it?" I asked. The thought of her touching Harry's mickey was horrifying. And why the hell would she want to blow on it?

"No! You eejit! She stuck it in her mouth and started to suck it!"

Jesus, Mary and Joseph! I felt sick. Father Murphy and my sister were right after all – the bloody English were a bunch of unholy perverts.

"Oh my sweet Jesus! Did you really say she stuck it in her mouth?"

Harry nodded.

"And she started to suck it?"

Harry nodded again.

My face was screwed up like I had just ate a lemon. I started spitting. It was like hearing your mother was a cannibal or something awful like that. My face stayed all screwed up for a few minutes as I imagined this. Harry just kept looking at the ground. Then after a while, I started to warm up to the possibilities of this "blow job" thing and a big smile broke across my face. We both looked at each other and burst out laughing.

I had a thousand questions for Harry, like when someone has an operation and you want to know all the gory details. Harry told me it felt nice, but he wasn't sure what he was supposed to do while she was down there, her head bopping up and down.

"What happens if you want to do a wee?" I asked.

This made Harry very thoughtful, so I knew the answer going to be good. He told me he thought I was on to something there and would have to think about it some more.

"I had to make her stop because her teeth kept hurting me," he confided.

"Jesus, was she trying to bite you?"

"Nah, it was just that her teeth were hurting me."

Then Harry went on to explain when he asked her to stop, she did something even more disgusting. I couldn't believe it could get more disgusting or interesting.

"She stopped and stood up…. and she fucken' tried to kiss me!"

"What the hell's wrong with that? I mean you were doing that all day, weren't you?"

"Yeah, but my mickey had just been in that mouth. Would you want to kiss a mouth that your mickey had just been in?"

I squirmed again and started spitting in earnest. Even Harry spat at this point.

"That Amanda is a holy disgrace. She must have no shame!"

None of the girls on our street would ever do anything like that. God knows what those English girls were up to.

Then I had another thought.

"How the hell did she learn that or what even made her think of it? Maybe she's the only girl in the world that does that... or maybe she invented it?"

Harry agreed that was a possibility because he'd never heard of it either.

"I saw a dog licking another dog's balls once," I volunteered.

Harry went a little pale as he told me that was something different, because he and Amanda were people.

"Dogs lick their own mickey?" I asked, trying to understand.

Harry gave me a clatter around the ear and told me he didn't like what I was implying.

"Anyway, she wasn't licking it; that would be disgusting. Amanda was sucking it. That's very, very different," he explained, getting angry.

Just then I had a brilliant thought that cleared up all the confusion.

"Maybe she was doing it all wrong, I mean it is called a 'blow job' right?"

Harry nodded in agreement.

"Don't you see? She was sucking it, not blowing it. I think she got confused." I concluded, pleased with my deduction.

Harry said he would think about that and made me swear not to tell anyone. I swore. Then I asked him why I fancied Bonny and not Amanda. He said he didn't fancy Bonny and we both agreed that this was amazing. Harry said that he felt there was some kind of law, a laws that we didn't know about yet, that makes us fancy one person and not another.

I knew Amanda was more like me and maybe that was why I didn't fancy her. I mean, you can't fancy anyone that reminds you of yourself. Amanda had the same kind of skin as me, the only difference was my mickey. Whereas, Bonny was a goddess, even her smell was different. Then a very bad thought crossed my mind; if I was so much like Amanda, Harry's mickey could have been in my mouth. I squirmed uncomfortably and spit, an extra big glob, to get rid of the thought.

Harry asked me what was wrong.

"Nuthin'."

What else could I say?

Then we went home for our tea. At the table with my mom, she asked me if I was all right because I looked a little pale. I believe in God and all his angels and that night they played a huge joke on me - we had sausages and mashed potatoes for dinner and I just sat there grinning from ear to ear, watching my sisters eat the big sausages on their forks. I burst out laughing at my big sister, who was eating the sausage sideways. She shot me a dirty look and asked me what I thought was so funny.

My mother looked at me from the corner of her eyes, in that certain way that made me ashamed. She seemed to know what I was thinking. Then I relaxed because how could she possibly know about such a dirty thing. Then some horrifying thoughts crossed my mind, "Could she know? Does she know?" I looked at her, shocked. This time, she really did know what I was thinking because she looked away, embarrassed.

My God, I thought. My mother knows about blow jobs.

THE PARTY

After dinner I went upstairs to get dressed. Everything was changing so fast. First there was Bonny and her bruise. Then there was Harry's "blow job." And now, it seemed my own father and mother may have done these unspeakable things.

I met up with Patsy, Derek, Pierce, Dermot and the lads from both ends of the street. We were all going to the party, and for most of us this was the first party we had ever been to. There was a lot of speculation about what we were in for. Patsy Whealan said he didn't care what was happening, but there was no way he was kissing any of them girls. Harry put him in his place by saying something about his bun in the oven not having risen. None of us knew what the hell he was talking about, so we all said nothing.

We all sauntered to Kathy's house as if we did this everyday of our lives. There was strange music playing. Later we found out it was called "rock and roll," imported from England by Bonny and Amanda. It was weird, some guy singing about a rock and a clock. The music was catchy and left a kind of feeling I hadn't felt before. My foot was tapping by itself, and I wanted to move to it in a funny way.

Bonny came over to me. She was wearing a pink dress which was so short I thought she forgot to put on her skirt.

"Hi Merwin," she said, smiling sweetly. She really looked pleased to see me.

This was so new to me. Everybody I knew in my life

was from my street, and they rarely looked happy to see me, unless I had sweets or something. But Bonny liked me for being me. She lifted me from my everyday hum-drum life in Ballyfermot to a place where I was "experiencing."

She took me by the hand into the parlor. I was a little frightened since I had no idea what she was going to do with me, especially with all the recent revelations I was having. There was a big couch in the corner, and she told me to sit down. Then she sat on my knee and put her arm around me. I must have looked like a deer caught in the headlights of a car.

"What's the matter, Merwin? Are you fwightened?"

I just shook my head.

I froze because she really seemed to know how all these things worked… and I was afraid she was planning one of those "blow job" things. She looked into my eyes as I anxiously watched for her next move. Then the door opened. Amanda and Kathy came in and told us to come out because the games were starting. When we were all herded into the living room, Amanda took charge and told us we were going to play "Postman's Knock."

"First someone has to go out into the hall with all the lights out. Mervyn, you go first." And I was ushered out into the hall.

"Now, Mervyn, knock on the door between one and eight times," Amanda said through the door. "Pick any number you want."

From the hallway, I knocked six times on the door. I heard squeals of laughter outside. Now, I wondered what I had just done.

"Theresa, it's you." I heard Amanda say. Then the door opened to whoops and laughter.

I could just make out Theresa Madden in the darkness of the hallway as she came over to me. She put her arms around me. She was one of the big girls from the "Other End," and I was surprised that she wanted to put her arms around me. She leaned forward, opened her mouth and stuck her tongue really far down my throat. I was disgusted and shocked, but I just stood there like a baby bird with its mouth wide open, being fed by its mother. She kept rolling her tongue inside my mouth. So this is french kissing. Now I understood what Harry and Amanda had been doing. She pulled back a little and looked at me, maybe to see how much I was enjoying it. Then she repeated the whole process. It was kind of like the doctor examining your mouth, without the blood and pain, so I just let her do it.

She seemed to be enjoying herself, and I was happy that I could add so much to somebody's pleasure. I saw that she was imagining things because her eyes were closed and she was making little moaning sounds. Actually, I think she forgot about me. This thing could have gone on indefinitely, as long as I kept my mouth opened. Then she gave me a big squeeze. I never squeezed a girl before and she felt nice. My mind started wandering and I wondered how long this would go on when on some invisible signal, she withdrew her tongue and gasped.

"Okay, now you go back into the room," she said.

I was dismissed. When I came out all the lads were looking at me, laughing and cheering and so were the girls. I couldn't believe Theresa, who was Irish and from our street, knew how to kiss like that. Where could she possibly have learned that and with who? I was surprised that all the girls from our street seemed to know this stuff. How come I didn't know this?

Theresa knocked on the door three times and everybody looked at Patsy.

"I'm not going in there!" he protested. "I'm not kissing Theresa Madden."

But Harry and Pierce grabbed him, opened the door and shoved him into the hall. I didn't have to imagine this, I knew how Theresa would grab and kiss him. Two minutes later, the door opened and Theresa came out looking like the cat that got the cream. She smiled at me. I think she meant something by the smile, but I didn't know how to read girls' smiles yet.

My head was racing with all these new impressions, so I hardly noticed that Patsy's knock brought in Amanda. Patsy came out real fast because he knew Harry wouldn't be pleased at all. My number was seven, so with each knock, I willed Amanda to stop. Unfortunately she did stop - at seven.

I went into the hallway and Amanda moved towards

me. I nearly blacked out, thinking about Amanda putting her tongue in my mouth, but thank God, she only kissed me on the cheek. It was strange, but Amanda and I knew there was some invisible universal law that prevented us from being attracted to each other. I made a mental note to read up on that. Besides, St. Mervyn appeared in my head and said, "That mouth had Harry Kennedy's mickey in it today." Before leaving, Amanda whispered, "Thank you, Mervyn."

Bonny had told me her number was five, so I knocked slowly five times. The door opened and in walked my Bonny. She stood on the first step of the stairs and held her arms out for me. She went straight for it. Her tongue went right into my mouth. I had some practice with Theresa, so I let myself enjoy this. It was a beautiful tongue. I felt weak with this new feeling, and I didn't care if this was wrong. I remember thinking, "to hell with sin" and kissed her back. Unlike with Theresa, this felt right. I closed my eyes really sincerely so Bonny would be impressed. I explored her soft fat juicy tongue with mine. It seemed more familiar than Theresa's. She moaned a little and I think I did too, just to show I wasn't stupid.

I don't know how long we were like that, but we were finally interrupted by a loud banging on the door and everybody shouting at us to hurry up. There was also a knock on the front door. I was holding Bonny with one arm and opened the hall door with the other.

It was the devil himself, in the form of my older sister.

She had a scowl on her face, indicating that I was seriously in the shit and she was going to make sure that I was going to pay for this. She looked at my arm around Bonny and her arm around me. You could see her brain working, as she seemed to sense the electric energy Bonny and I had created in the hall.

"What are you doing to my brother?" she growled at Bonny.

"We were just talking," I lied.

And as if right on cue, the door to the living room swung open, and Patsy asked real loud if us two love birds were finished yet. Then he saw my sister on the steps and froze.

"Get home right now you dirty little bastard!" she yelled, pointing across the street to our house. "And, you, stay away from my brother. You! English slag! He's only a child and not ready for the likes of you!"

I knew she was possessed by the devil. Even if she tried, she couldn't have said anything worse. I was so mortified that I just ran, crying, back home. That stupid cow had just ruined my life. How could I ever look Bonny in the face again.

At home, the whole family got involved, as my demon sister ratted me out.

"Ma, I caught that big fella kissing one of them English slags over in Kathy's hall. He's a dirty bastard and shouldn't be allowed out on the street again."

My mother looked at me and then at me da. My da looked at me and then at me ma. Then they both looked at me, as if I were a monster that had eaten Mervyn and rolled around in pigshit.

"Go up to bed. Now!" my ma shouted, pointing upstairs.

I knew she was saving me from my da. He was a slow thinker and me ma was much faster. She was getting me out of the room before he worked it out that he was going to kill me. I was up the stairs and into bed like a shot.

They were arguing downstairs, and I hoped me ma could keep the lid on things.

I listened for a while and thought about the look on Bonny's face when my sister called her an English slag. I remembered all the stuff we were taught in school about the horrible things that the British did to us in Ireland. But that wasn't Bonny's fault, was it?

I was caught in a whirlwind of thoughts and emotions. I had been flying high. Now I was falling really fast into the reality of being Irish and twelve with awful sisters and in love. How could something so great turn so terrible, so quickly? I was even in trouble with my parents, all because of Bonny's beautiful bruise on her beautiful arse, her sweet lisp and too big tongue. Life is so unfair. If my sister died when she was a kid, everything would have been better. Then I could have finished my kiss and snuck home, avoiding this mess. I heard my stupid sister coming up the stairs. She stuck her head in our bedroom and sneered, calling out, "dirty little bastard." My little brother, John, and I shared a bed; he slept through it all.

I turned on my side and thought of Bonny. We kissed and I felt this warm lovely feeling coming over me. Then we were lying in the park. I put my hand on her leg and slowly moved it up her skirt. There were no thoughts now about why I was doing anything; I was just doing it. Bonny turned to me as we began to squeeze each other. I started to kiss her ears and all over her face. I didn't know passion could be like this.

My hands were now firmly around her as she started to wriggle a bit, but I was much stronger and just held her tighter. The urge to touch her was so intense that I put my hand down her back and slipped my hands into her knickers. She was wiggling in ecstasy as I squeezed her bum. I tried to stick my tongue in her mouth. I was going mad with passion, and the more she wriggled, the more I was spurred on. It was time to plunge my hand down the front of her knickers. This was the moment.

Her moaning turned into shouting and screaming, and I was very confused. Then I heard my mother screaming and my little brother, terrified, screaming for our ma. I was still confused. Then I realized what I'd been doing in my sleep. I had my hands down my brother's underwear, and I was kissing him all over his face. He was kicking and screaming, trying to get my hand off his crotch and me off of him.

It was pretty surreal. In slow motion my mother was beating me over the head, my da was rushing up the stairs and my big sister was standing in her nightdress screaming that I had gone mad. I looked down and saw the terrified look on my brother's face. Then I saw that me ma was trying to drag me off my brother. I saw me da punch me in the head as he pulled me to the floor. As he began to kick the shit out of me, I finally came back to reality.

It's funny that when you're in mortal danger, you seem to have the time to observe things that you'd never normally think about. Maybe Eamon really had run in slow motion when he ran into the lamppost. Thank God me da had his shoes off. I even caught me ma's indecision as she was torn between comforting my shocked brother or saving me from certain death at the hands of me da. I suppose something kicks in when you're in danger. I even remembered letting me da belt me for what I did, but now he was really hurting me. He was going past some point and was going to kill me. Lying on the floor and getting kicked makes you "experience the roses," too. Can you believe that?

In slow motion, I saw my foot going up into me da's crotch and lifting his body off the floor. He sailed in slow motion out the door and down the stairs. I saw disbelief on me ma's face, my sister slowly crashing against the wall and my brother looking at me in a way that told me nothing would be ever the same again in our house. Now I was fully awake, on my feet, and completely alert. The immediate threat to my life was over.

Downstairs, I heard me da moaning and threatening me, but somehow I was no longer afraid of him. I reminded myself that I was now bigger and stronger than him.

But St. Mervyn appeared again and reprimanded me, "How could you do those things to your little brother, your father, that lovely English girl, your sister and your mother? You're a disgrace to the Catholic Church."

I was crying now, very hard, while hugging my mother. How did this nightmare happen? I had been gloriously in love and now I was a pervert and a dirty bastard. The twins had woken up. They'd heard about me groping John and came into the room to see what they were missing. One of them started to laugh.

You know when you're a kid and you know you're not supposed to laugh, so you do? Then the more you try to stop, you can't? Suddenly, one by one, everybody in the room started to laugh, not just laugh, but laugh hysterically. I looked over at John. He was last to start laughing, but I could see the relief on his face as he saw that everyone thought it was funny. Now he could get over it.

Everyone, that is, except for me da. The grumbling from the bottom of the stairs warned us that he wasn't affected by the laughter. Then me ma ran down after him. I learned later that he was all right, but he was going to hold a grudge for a long time. We didn't speak to each other for a few months, which was fine by me.

Anyway, that's how I got my very own bed and my brother had to sleep with me da.

* * *

STUDENT STORY: PIA
THE BLUE GLANCE OF THE SOUL

I want to share with you my first moment with Mervyn...

On March 2nd, 2006, a small group of students from the Mexico City School and New York School was on its way to Coatepec. I was full of anticipation on that Friday – finally, I would meet that wonderful man, a conscious man, of whom I had heard many things. Everyone was already seated when I arrived at the restaurant. Mervyn was at the end of the table. As soon as I saw him, my heart leaped and I felt it might jump out of my chest. I didn't know what to do, I was very happy but a little nervous too, so I whispered a shy, "hello" and avoided his gaze. That afternoon, I attended the lecture he gave on "Love and the Soul". It was afternoon full of moments and sensations that I can't quite put into words.

The following day, Mervyn gave a lecture on the "Beginning of the Universe and Body Types" at the central patio of a colonial hotel in Coatepec. That day, the beautiful old stone columns surrounding a fountain, the flowers, the carved furniture and the light crossing the stained glass windows became a holy place. After listening to him, we were filled with a deep joy and an understanding

219

that we had found the path to a strange and beautiful journey. Then and there, we toasted to the birth of the Xalapa School. Later, we, as new students, had our first meal together as a School. And then, Mervyn and I had our first Moment.

The sounds disappeared....everything became silent for me. His Blue Glance invited me to share... to live...to feel... a moment of eternity. I was unable to move. I melted in his gaze. Feeling such lightness... I grew and grew... larger than my body ... larger than the building... taller than the domes of the nearby church... an indescribable expansion....a gigantic heart in peace. Ahhhhh! I stayed there... I don't know for how long... until little by little I could "fit" inside myself again.

Tears from a secret spring, full of the most profound gratitude, started flowing. They were not salty, they were pure and free. No knot in my throat. They were a thank you without words... tears born of a new heart... a renewed covenant... sealed forever by the eternal memory of Mervyn's clear glance... and the soft movement of his lips... when they silently formed the words... "thank you".

With Love,
Pia

* * *

10
ACROSS THE IRISH SEA

Mervyn passed away before he finished this book. Among his manuscripts were notes to himself to add certain anecdotes and messages. He planned to conclude his childhood memoir with a story about leaving Ireland. This story was the symbolic end to his childhood and entrance into his adult life.

While editing and organizing his stories, we recognized that Mervyn's unwritten chapter was integral to his book. So it was decided that one of Mervyn's oldest students and friends would conclude his memoir. Irish by birth and living in England, Rylie met Mervyn when she was eighteen. It was a very difficult time in her life and his friendship and guidance would anchor her spiritual growth for the years to come. She wrote this last chapter in Mervyn's voice, inspired by her memories of our teacher and guided by his Spirit.

ACROSS THE IRISH SEA

At the age of sixteen, I left Ireland. My whole body felt heavy with sadness as I held onto the cold rails of the ferry. I watched through tears as the horseshoe bay of Dublin disappeared into the mist and sea. Life is like a big book full of little events and chapters, but you can never go back to them again, except in memory. With the Irish Sea surrounding me, propelling me into a new unknown chapter, I slowly turned like a compass towards England, my new home.

I wasn't alone in my decision to leave Ireland. Countless numbers of young, hopeful people filed onto the boats each day and sailed towards England. Like me, most of them were trying their luck in London. There are invisible forces that push people to move in different directions or change their circumstances: money is a big one, sometimes it's babies, then there's sex. I found consolation in the middle of this sadness knowing that there were thousands of gorgeous English girls waiting for me on the other side.

I began to look around at the others on the ferry. I was just one in a crowd, yet I felt something else looking through them and through me, like sunlight peering through the translucent almost-full moon hanging softly in the sky. Seagulls circled and soared triumphantly in the wind, their invisible master. One seagull floated in the sky completely motionless, wings outstretched. "Did past or future exist in such freedom?" I thought, deep within myself.

Suddenly that soaring bird became a kite string tied into my heart. That familiar feeling of "experiencing the roses" was happening again. My heart swelled with a love greater, far greater, than the sea. How could such a small organ in my chest hold such intense love? In the depths of my heart, a kernel of certainty vibrated with the deep joy of knowing. Ireland and all my loved ones, now so distant, were as much a part of me as my hands and feet were part of my body.

The crowd around me became like stars in the universe. I felt a sublime love for every person. Time no longer existed; everything around me spiraled into me, into my soul. Then the eye of this magnificent storm swelled love as it surged outwards in ever widening circles. God must wield a great branding iron. It was searing something divine and timeless inside me. All my thoughts and memories were like sparks from a match. Was it possible that one small person could catch God's attention?

My hand moved to my pocket, I felt the crinkled notes and loose change, and pulled out a picture. It was six-year-old me in my Sunday best grinning obediently. Was I ever really this boy? Then I gasped. I felt as if every atom exploded through my body, mind and heart, like the waves crashing around me. "Let go! Let go!" they laughed. I felt the invisible Father guiding me. This love was too big for me, it filled the universe – maybe loving our fellow man is the key to this world? The words of Jesus echoed, "I am in the Father and He is in me." This love could not be held in one man. Love was a sacred gift from a sacred visitor and it sealed something eternal inside me.

I looked down and saw the small beaten up suitcase me ma had found in the attic. I heard her voice and was reminded once again of the other me, the mortal me. "Don't be bringin' any of those socks with holes with ya!" I cringed in realization that me ma would never be able to see me as a man. Perhaps this fragile human form returns again and again to experience and transform our memories into a movie, an offering to God at one's death?

Well, I was human again, just one of the hopeful immigrants trying their luck in London. I shivered and hunched up against the cold rain that started to beat down. I was well used to a bit of rain, but me ma had warned me not to get my suit wet – it was made of the best Donegal wool and would shrink.

Suddenly I was taken by a beautiful vision - a beautiful girl with red hair, a pale freckled face with the greenest eyes. I looked behind me but she was definitely heading for me!

"Hello," she sang sweetly, "my name is Angie. Would you like to share me umbrella till we get on dry land?"

I felt like a deer caught in the headlights. I smiled brightly and nodded obediently like the little boy in the picture. I remembered the little boy at the bus stop in Dublin hoping to share an umbrella with a girl—hadn't that been a dream? Now it was happening for real!

An enormous wall of white cliffs appeared as we pulled

into Dover. The hand that writes moves on and new chapters lay ahead of me. Like an actor, I prepared to take my place on the new stage. It would take my entire life to learn about the frailties of human love and the promise of Divine Love - but this journey is our birthright, it is the sacred journey of us all.

* * *

STUDENT STORY: CHRISTIAN
THE GIFT OF PRESENCE

I met Mervyn when Annamaria first invited me to see her teacher.

He asked me, "Do you believe we have a Soul?"

In that moment I felt Mervyn's Presence and it moved me to the point where I couldn't stop crying. After departing, I had this incredible feeling of finding "magic" and in my heart I knew I had found my school.

After seven years, I can say that the Academy is not only my school, but something more like my home.

Christian

* * *

INTERVIEW WITH MERVYN 1999-2000

Q: Your teachings suggests a history in the West of spiritual seeking that perhaps has gone unacknowledged by comparison to what is commonly accepted as the spiritual wealth of the East. You offer interpretations of Western art, particularly of Italian Renaissance and Pre-Raphaelite paintings, as well as poetry, fairytales, and essays on Western mysticism and its history. Why is the immense wealth of Western spirituality over the centuries from Plato to present so little known or understood?

Mervyn Brady: In the East, a man could sit under a tree and declare himself enlightened or awake and people would be very happy, feed and support him, and there would be those would wish to become his pupils. In the West, the church had a monopoly on God and ruled with an iron fist. If one tried to reach God any other way than their way, one would risk being burned alive. However, common sense would indicate that when one looks at the evolution of Europe compared with the East, there simply must have been conscious and awake men behind it. It is unlikely ordinary men could have created perhaps the most sophisticated society in the history of man.

Schools were there, but for safety, hid themselves very deeply from the prying eyes of the church. Some were in fact so successful they even existed within the church itself. In each case, these schools had to find ways to transmit their ideas, and they invariably used various art forms. For example, the Medicis in Florence who produced Leonardo da Vinci, Botticelli, etc. What is generally not known is that these men were philosophers first and their art was a way for them to express and hide their findings.

They were so successful at this that until now even scholars have not realized the implications and hidden meanings in their various paintings. For example, the Mona Lisa: The strange expression on her face is in reality the expression of a human being in the mystical state in which the soul looks out through the eyes and not with them. In order to paint such a picture, Leonardo da Vinci would have to be very familiar with this state.

Q: What is the basis of your philosophy?

MB: That man is asleep. When a human is born, there is a

body and a Soul, which share space 50/50 until the age of three. At that point, the body starts to become more and more active, learning its name, all about its surroundings, parental influence, even the country it comes from. The Soul is constantly pushed into the background, and, through lack of stimulation, begins to fall asleep. By the time a person has reached age seven, this process is normally complete; the soul is asleep and its influence divorced from the body.

Most people live their whole lives in this condition unless some external shock is applied to the body (i.e. the death of a close friend). Such a shock awakens the Soul and one may then turn to higher orders and begin to ask questions. However, the body is designed to put the Soul back to sleep as it will not share the space readily with an apparent intruder. For some people, however, either the Soul does not completely go to sleep in the first place, or there is sufficient friction to reduce the power of the body and allow the Soul to slowly open its eyes. Our school would be designed for someone like this, or in this condition. Schools such as ours have come not to awaken, but to provide water to those who thirst, and direction to those who are lost.

Q: What is the awakening of the Soul and what is required?

MB: The awakening of the Soul is exactly what the words say. The Soul awakens and has to find a way to manifest in this world. However, the body will constantly try to take this space and claim it for its own. It is interesting that we have a Soul, but we don't always remember that. Therefore, the first requirement is to "remember" the Soul. This is man's greatest obstacle; he forgets and becomes consumed by the body's attempts to digest and control his life. A man must find a way to constantly "remember" his inner world.

Q: What role does literature and art play in spiritual awakening?

MB: European schools left their teachings in various art forms. Most people don't realize fairytales, for example, came from schools and contain precise descriptions of the interplay between body and Soul. Paintings contain lessons, which those who have learned the various symbols can decipher. Bach called cathedrals "petrified music." An instructed man can "read" a cathedral and see the meanings of gargoyles, form and ritual.

Q: Does this differ from eastern beliefs or traditional Western Christianity?

MB: Yes, the East did not develop man's emotions to the level that Western schools did. Eastern art remains simple. Simple and elegant, but its music has not produced a Mozart, or its painting, a Raphael. When the Soul of a man awakens and wishes to communicate with fellow Souls, great objective art is produced.

Regarding traditional Western Christianity, most of the art was mass-produced and dictated by the church. However, esoteric schools created objective art, which is far higher and contains hidden treats generally unknown to traditional art.

Q: Your teachings highlight main historical figures in western history including Plato, Da Vinci, Raphael, Shakespeare, Elizabeth I, St. Teresa of Avila, Goethe, Blake and Walt Whitman. What is it about these people and their works you feel is important to understand?

MB: Each of the people you have mentioned, and there are many more, have reached a point where their Soul awoke and manifested. Each one of them left a map of how they achieved this spiritual awakening, and the obstacles they incurred along the way. Surely, to study Goethe, Whitman, etc., would produce gems of understanding unrealized by most new age teachings.

Q: Your teachings emphasize themes of love and spiritual awakening. You seem to suggest that a strong connection exists between the two, both positive and negative, and that you feel there is a great deal of misunderstanding about love, sex and spirituality. Can you further explain the connection, including what role you feel sex plays in life and spirituality?

MB: There are many levels and obstacles that a person has to overcome on the long journey to find the Holy Grail, or spiritual awakening. We see that even with Sir Lancelot, although he was a great knight full of prowess and possibilities, his weakness in the sexual arena prevented him from finding what he was seeking. When a person is quite a reasonable distance down this road, it is then that sex and love rise to test him. Without preparation or proper instruction, most people would be sidetracked or even stopped dead in their tracks by these powerful forces.

I have seen many fine people spiritually ripening, only to be consumed and stopped by the lower part of the love experience. On the positive side, it is the energy generated by this experience that, like for Dante with Beatrice, can propel a person into the higher realms. For most people, the experience of love invariably awakens the Soul and perhaps is what makes the state so desirable. It is because of the arrival of the Soul that lovers become content with the most simple things, such as a spring day and the sound of birds singing. There is an awareness and an energy generated that is not available to a person in their day to day life. For some people, losing a loved one simultaneously means losing the connection with their inner world. A true philosopher would be a person who seeks within and not without for their missing half. When one finds one's own Soul, love in its highest form manifests. It is only when one has experienced this love that one can truly love others.

MESSAGE TO ACADEMY, JUNE 2001

Dear All,

The Academy is changing.

The event for which we have been preparing for such a long and interesting time is slowly sliding into being--like waking up one day and realising one is an adult.

Somewhere there was an invisible membrane dividing childhood and adulthood, and suddenly, without warning, you have moved from one to the other.

The Academy is different. It is no longer the school we started so many years ago.

I remember saying to a small group of people, "You have no idea

what is being conceived here tonight."
We have been given more abilities since then… and I do believe that the Gods are close.

I trust they are pleased with their work.
For I know that nothing could have been different… Nothing.

I have watched as each of you over the years has been carved from your original shells and I have been honoured to watch your unfolding.

I have learned so much from you all by learning to see through your senses, and feeling your feelings both joyful and sorrowful.

The hard work of splitting in the dark underground like a seed has been done and we have prevailed into the light. We are now like the plant growing, and soon something of indescribable beauty will emerge.

Our Flowering, followed in due course by our Fragrance.
I want to thank you all, for your part in this most divine play.

Love,
Mervyn

* * *

THE END.
AND THE BEGINNING…

MEMORATE TE SEMPER

The Academy of European Arts and Culture has centers in
the United States, Mexico, the United Kingdom & Australia.
If you would like more information about the Academy,
please visit:

Mexico
www.academiadearteseuropeas.mx

U.K.
www.academyofeuropeanarts.co.uk

U.S.
www.academyofeuropeanarts.com

www.ingramcontent.com/pod-product-compliance
Lightning Source LLC
Chambersburg PA
CBHW031510040426
42445CB00009B/159